First World War
and Army of Occupation
War Diary
France, Belgium and Germany

35 DIVISION
Headquarters, Branches and Services
Royal Army Veterinary Corps
Assistant Director Veterinary Services
1 February 1916 - 17 April 1919

WO95/2473/3

The Naval & Military Press Ltd
www.nmarchive.com
Published in association with The National Archives

Published by

The Naval & Military Press Ltd

Unit 10 Ridgewood Industrial Park,

Uckfield, East Sussex,

TN22 5QE England

Tel: +44 (0) 1825 749494

www.naval-military-press.com

www.nmarchive.com

This diary has been reprinted in facsimile from the original. Any imperfections are inevitably reproduced and the quality may fall short of modern type and cartographic standards.

© Crown Copyright
Images reproduced by permission of The National Archives, London, England, 2015.

Contents

Document type	Place/Title	Date From	Date To
Heading	WO95/2473/3 35 Div Feb'16-Apr'19 Ass. Director Vet. Services.		
Heading	35th Division Divl Troops. A.D. Veterinary Services Feb 1916-Apr 1919		
War Diary	Havre	01/02/1916	03/02/1916
War Diary	St. Omer	04/02/1916	04/02/1916
War Diary	Le Nieppe	05/02/1916	09/02/1916
War Diary	Lambres	10/02/1916	18/02/1916
War Diary	Lestrem	19/02/1916	29/02/1916
Heading	A.D.V.S. Vol. 2. 35 Div.		
War Diary	Lestrem	01/03/1916	28/03/1916
War Diary	Sailly	29/03/1916	20/04/1916
War Diary	Lestrem	21/04/1916	31/05/1916
Miscellaneous	35 D/1459/A. Appendix I.	02/05/1916	02/05/1916
War Diary	Lestrem	01/06/1916	17/06/1916
War Diary	Busnes	18/06/1916	02/07/1916
War Diary	Doullens	03/07/1916	07/07/1916
War Diary	Bus-Les Artois	08/07/1916	09/07/1916
War Diary	Contay	10/07/1916	12/07/1916
War Diary	Morlancourt	13/07/1916	05/08/1916
War Diary	Cavillon	06/08/1916	09/08/1916
War Diary	Corbie	10/08/1916	15/08/1916
War Diary	Citadel	16/08/1916	25/08/1916
War Diary	Forked-Tree	26/08/1916	29/08/1916
War Diary	Doullens	30/08/1916	01/09/1916
War Diary	Le Cauroy	02/09/1916	06/09/1916
War Diary	Duisans	07/09/1916	05/12/1916
War Diary	Roellecourt	06/12/1916	05/02/1917
War Diary	Bouquemaison	06/02/1917	06/02/1917
War Diary	Vignacourt	07/02/1917	17/02/1917
War Diary	Guillaucourt	18/02/1917	21/02/1917
War Diary	Caix	22/02/1917	17/03/1917
War Diary	Rosieres	18/03/1917	28/03/1917
War Diary	Nesle	29/03/1917	11/04/1917
War Diary	Monchy-Lagache	12/04/1917	22/05/1917
War Diary	Peronne	23/05/1917	24/05/1917
War Diary	Gurlu-Wood	25/05/1917	08/07/1917
War Diary	Villers-Faucon.	09/07/1917	02/10/1917
War Diary	Duisans	03/10/1917	12/10/1917
War Diary	Lederzeele	13/10/1917	16/10/1917
War Diary	J Camp, International Corner	17/10/1917	17/10/1917
War Diary	J. Camp.	18/10/1917	27/10/1917
War Diary	J. Camp.	28/11/1917	31/11/1917
War Diary	J. Camp. International Corner.	01/11/1917	04/11/1917
War Diary	J. Camp.	05/11/1917	05/11/1917
War Diary	Proven	06/11/1917	16/11/1917
War Diary	Border Camp	17/11/1917	10/12/1917
War Diary	Couthove Chateau	11/12/1917	21/12/1917
War Diary	Couthove	22/12/1917	09/01/1918
War Diary	Welsh Farm.	10/01/1918	28/01/1918

War Diary	Canal Bank.	29/01/1918	31/01/1918
War Diary	Canal-Bank C:25.c.75 Sheet 28	01/02/1918	06/02/1918
War Diary	Canal-Bank	07/02/1918	07/02/1918
War Diary	Elverdinghe	08/02/1918	10/03/1918
War Diary	St. Sixte.	11/03/1918	23/03/1918
War Diary	Mericourt Sur Somme	24/03/1918	24/03/1918
War Diary	Bray-Sur-Somme	25/03/1918	25/03/1918
War Diary	Henencourt	26/03/1918	30/03/1918
War Diary	Pont Noyelles	31/03/1918	06/04/1918
War Diary	Puchevillers	07/04/1918	08/04/1918
War Diary	Toutencourt	09/04/1918	17/04/1918
Miscellaneous	Effects Of Mustard Gas		
Miscellaneous	Mustard Gas. Appendix A.	18/04/1918	18/04/1918
War Diary	Toutencourt	18/04/1918	25/04/1918
Miscellaneous	Succeed Calie Poisoning Caster Oil Beans.		
War Diary	Toutencourt	26/04/1918	05/05/1918
War Diary	Herissart	06/05/1918	20/05/1918
War Diary	Toutencourt	21/05/1918	07/06/1918
Miscellaneous	Sholing Wear of Shols		
War Diary	Toutencourt	08/06/1918	10/06/1918
Miscellaneous	Rabies no Appendix attached.		
War Diary	Toutencourt	11/06/1918	16/06/1918
War Diary	Beauquesne	17/06/1918	30/06/1918
War Diary	Beauquesne & Wizernes	01/07/1918	01/07/1918
War Diary	Oudezeele	02/07/1918	05/07/1918
War Diary	Q.11.a.2.8 (Sheet 27)	06/07/1918	11/07/1918
War Diary	Terdeghem	12/07/1918	09/08/1918
War Diary	Cassell	10/08/1918	01/09/1918
War Diary	Herzeele	02/09/1918	03/09/1918
War Diary	Vogeltje	04/09/1918	16/09/1918
War Diary	Waratah Farm	17/09/1918	19/09/1918
War Diary	Waratah Farm 28/G.15.a.6.0	20/09/1918	24/09/1918
War Diary	Waratah Farm.	25/09/1918	29/09/1918
War Diary	Assam.	30/09/1918	30/09/1918
War Diary	Assam Farm 28/H.22.a.2.7	01/10/1918	08/10/1918
War Diary	Assam Farm	09/10/1918	17/10/1918
War Diary	Poeselhoek	18/10/1918	20/10/1918
War Diary	Marcke	21/10/1918	23/10/1918
War Diary	Courtrai	24/10/1918	27/10/1918
War Diary	Sweveghem.	28/10/1918	06/11/1918
War Diary	St. Louis.	07/11/1918	10/11/1918
War Diary	Quaremont	11/11/1918	17/11/1918
War Diary	Harlebeke	18/11/1918	30/11/1918
Miscellaneous	To Hd. Qtrs 35 Div.	01/01/1919	01/01/1919
War Diary	Eperlecques	01/12/1918	29/03/1919
War Diary	Tilques	30/03/1919	17/04/1919

WO95/2473
35 Div
Feb '16 - Apr '19
Ass. Director Vet. Services

③

35TH DIVISION
DIVL TROOPS

A. D. VETERINARY SERVICES
FEB 1916-APR 1919

WAR DIARY of A.D.V.S. 35th Division. Army Form C. 2118

or

INTELLIGENCE SUMMARY

(Erase heading not required.)

Place	Date	Hour	Summary of Events and Information	Remarks and references to Appendices
HAVRE	1.2.16	9 am	Disembarked at port of HAVRE with Divisional Cavalry + 45th Mobile Veterinary Section.	Feb '16
"	2.2.16		Remaining at HAVRE.	
		9 am	Received instructions to entrain at port 3, HAVRE at 11.59 am.	
HAVRE	3.2.16	11 am	Took over charge of train + received instructions from R.T.O. for journey.	ap.19
		5 p.m.	Watered + fed horses at MONTEROLIER – BUCHY.	
ST.OMER	4.2.16	6.30 am	Arrival at ST.OMER.	
		9.30 am	Motored to Divisional Head Quarters at LE NIEPPE. Arranged Veterinary charge for all Reports arrival to D.V.S. units of the Division.	
LE NIEPPE	5.2.16	9 am	Inspected Divisional Cavalry. The majority of horses in the open; condition good; a few cases of catarrh, otherwise no sickness. Horses very muddy.	

Army Form C. 2118

WAR DIARY
or
INTELLIGENCE SUMMARY

(Erase heading not required.)

Instructions regarding War Diaries and Intelligence Summaries are contained in F. S. Regs., Part II. and the Staff Manual respectively. Title Pages will be prepared in manuscript.

Place	Date	Hour	Summary of Events and Information	Remarks and references to Appendices
LE NIEPPE	5.2.16	11 am	Inspected 105th Infantry Brigade; majority of animals under cover; a few cases of catarrh but otherwise good.	
"			Drafted from we horses left on lines of march, for inclusion in Divisional Orders.	
"	6.2.16	10 am	Inspected all units in 106th Brigade Area; animals in good condition; a few cases of catarrh among the horses of the Train.	
"	7.2.16		Inspected units in 104th Brigade Area; condition good; about 50% animals under shelter. Instructed O.C. No 2 C.A.V.C. to send 3 horses to Mobile Veterinary Section.	
"	8.2.16	10 am	Inspected Head Quarters C.W.A.S.C: a few cases of catarrh among the H.D. horses. Lines very muddy + recommended removal to a better standing.	

Army Form C. 2118

WAR DIARY
or
INTELLIGENCE SUMMARY
(Erase heading not required.)

Instructions regarding War Diaries and Intelligence Summaries are contained in F. S. Regs., Part II. and the Staff Manual respectively. Title Pages will be prepared in manuscript.

Place	Date	Hour	Summary of Events and Information	Remarks and references to Appendices
LE NIEPPE	9.2.16	9.30 am	Proceeded from LE NIEPPE to LAMBRES to change of Divisional Head Quarters.	
		2 pm.	Provided Veterinary charge for all units of the Division in the new area.	
		3 pm.	D.D.V.S. 1st Army called at Office and left certain instructions for guidance & 8 horses evacuated by M.V.1.	
LAMBRES	10.2.16	10 am	Inspected 163rd Agricult. Bn. at MARTHES; horses in good condition; few casualties; horses lines muddy.	
		12 Nm	Inspected 35th D.A.C. at MAMETZ; Horses & mules in good condition; few casualties; lines very muddy.	
		3 pm.	Interviewed V.O. to 158th Bde. R.F.A. with reference to 12 horses left at HERBELLE	
		4 pm.	Visited M.V.1 at QUERNES. in new area.	

1875 Wt. W593/826 1,000,000 4/15 J.B.C. & A. A.D.S.S./Forms/C. 2118.

Army Form C. 2118

WAR DIARY
or
INTELLIGENCE SUMMARY
(Erase heading not required.)

Instructions regarding War Diaries and Intelligence Summaries are contained in F. S. Regs., Part II. and the Staff Manual respectively. Title Pages will be prepared in manuscript.

Place	Date	Hour	Summary of Events and Information	Remarks and references to Appendices
LAMBRES	11.2.16		Routine work.	
"	12.2.16		Inspected 106th Infantry Bde. Horses under cover; Mules in open & lines very muddy. Health good; feet & few casualties.	
			Inspected 205° C. R. E: animals in the open; health & condition good.	
"		3 P.M.	Inspected sick animals with M.V.1.	
"	13.2.16		Routine work.	
"	14.2.16		Inspected 104th Infantry Brigade: majority of animals under cover. Health good & few casualties; condition of animal good; lines very wet & muddy.	
			Inspected No. 2 C. A.T.C.: Animals in open; health & condition good.	
		3 P.M.	Called at Office of D.D.V.1. 1st Army.	

WAR DIARY
or
INTELLIGENCE SUMMARY
(Erase heading not required.)

Army Form C. 2118

Place	Date	Hour	Summary of Events and Information	Remarks and references to Appendices
LAMBRES	15.2.16	2 p.m.	Inspected 204th F.C. R.E.: Animals in open; conditions of animals good.	
"	"	"	No 3. C. A.C.C.: Horses in open; conditions + health good.	
"	"	"	106th Ft. Ambulance; Horses mostly under cover; condition + health good.	
"	16.2.16	11 am	Proceeded to LESTREM to interview A.D.V.S. 30th Division re move of Division into his area.	
"	17.2.16		Proceeded to LA HAYE to arrange to take over billets for M.V.S. from the 19th Div.	
"	18.2.16		Proceeded to LESTREM on change of Divisional Head Quarters. Provided Veterinary charge for all units in the new area.	
LESTREM	19.2.16		Inspected animals of West Yorkshire Bgn: Health + condition good; Sent one horse had nonies to M.V.S. for evacuation.	

Army Form C. 2118

WAR DIARY
or
INTELLIGENCE SUMMARY
(Erase heading not required.)

Place	Date	Hour	Summary of Events and Information	Remarks and references to Appendices
LESTREM	20.12.16		Inspected No.1.6. Divisional Horses at LE SART. 50 ?, 8 horses under cover. Health & condition good. Evacuated 2 horses to M.V.1.	
		12 Non	Inspected 157" Bgde. R.F.A.: Condition of horses generally good; a few horses of Ammunition Column in light condition; health generally good. Inries very mangey.	
			Visited Mobile Veterinary Section at LA HAYE.	
		3.30	Arranged with A.D.V.S. 30" Div. to provide Veterinary care of 105" Infantry Bde. whilst attached to his Division.	
" "	21.12.16		Interviewed V.Os. i/c 158" Bde. & 163" Bde. with reference to horses left in last billeting area.	
		5 P.M.	Visited Mobile Veterinary Section.	

WAR DIARY
or
INTELLIGENCE SUMMARY
(Erase heading not required.)

Army Form C. 2118

Place	Date	Hour	Summary of Events and Information	Remarks and references to Appendices
LESTREM	22.2.16		Routine work.	
"	23.2.16		Inspected 105th & 107th F. Ambulances with V.6 sp. Majority of animals made covers. Health & condition good.	
			Inspected No. 2 C.M.T.C. 50% of animals made covers. One horse badly kicked. Health & condition good.	
			Inspected 18th & 20th Lancashire Familiars. Health & condition good. Many made shelters.	
"	24.2.16	10 am	Inspected M.V.J.	
		11 am	Inspected 203 & 204th F. C. R. E.: Animals in the open; condition & health very good.	
			Inspected 106th F. Ambulance: Animals made covers; no casualties: health & condition good.	

WAR DIARY or INTELLIGENCE SUMMARY

Army Form C. 2118

Place	Date	Hour	Summary of Events and Information	Remarks and references to Appendices
LESTREM	24.2.16		Inspected 23rd Manchester & 17th Lancashire Fusiliers: Animals mostly under cover: health & condition good: few consultations. Inspected Signal Co. Animals in open on hard standings: condition fair: health good. Hard feet & sore shoulders common.	
"	25.2.16		Conference of all V.Os at M.V.I. at LA HAYE. Issued elastic tourniquets to all V.Os.	
"		2 pm	Inspected 205 F. Co. R.E. at LE SART. Health good: Animals mostly in the open.	
"	26.2.16		Inspected No. 1 Co. A.T.C.: 50% horses in open: health & condition good. Phr. transport of N.Z.Y. & 106th Bde. H.Q.: Animals under shelter: condition good. Hard feet & sore shoulders present Back.	

WAR DIARY
or
INTELLIGENCE SUMMARY

Army Form C. 2118

Place	Date	Hour	Summary of Events and Information	Remarks and references to Appendices
ESTREM	27.2.16		Inspected No. 3 Co. Divisional Train: Animals in open: Health & condition good.	
"	28.2.16	10 am	Visited A.5. M.V.T. Inspected 150th F.A. Brigade. This unit met & recently after the Thaw. Horses in Ammunition Column in light condition. Horses of batteries in fair condition. Health generally good.	
"	29.2.16		Arranged for Veterinary care of Ammn. Col. of 2nd Indian Royal Horse Artillery & 47th Reserve Park whilst our orders are moving for 150th Bde. Interviewed D.A.D.O.S. re MERVILLE STN.	
		11.30 am	Inspected M.V.T. entraining and horses at MERVILLE STN.	

ADVS
vol 2
issue 3

WAR DIARY of A.D.V.S. 35th Div.

or

INTELLIGENCE SUMMARY

(Erase heading not required.)

Army Form C. 2118

Instructions regarding War Diaries and Intelligence Summaries are contained in F. S. Regs., Part II. and the Staff Manual respectively. Title Pages will be prepared in manuscript.

Place	Date	Hour	Summary of Events and Information	Remarks and references to Appendices
LESTREM	1.3.16	3 PM	All V.Os of Division attended a demonstration of Intra-dermal palpebral method of mallein testing by D.D.V.S. 1st Army at LA HAYE. A full account of operation, results, advantages, re new serum and afterwards all V.Os performed the operation. Winter mild.	
"	2.3.16	9 am	Proceeded to 159th Bty. R.F.A. and inspected the horses of the brigade with V.O. Majority of horses in the open; picket lines very muddy. Horses of batteries in good condition. Some horses of Ammunition Column in light condition: O.C. of Column reported shortage of hay – reported this to O.C. Brigade. Instructed V.O. to evacuate 7 cows to M.V.S.	
"	3.3.16	9 am	Inspected 163rd Howit. Brigade. A & B batteries : A few horses in light condition. C & D " : horses in good condition. Amm. Col. : condition good. Health generally good; few evacuations. Horses picketed on hard standings. Instructed V.O. to evacuate 7 cows to M.V.S.	

WAR DIARY
or
INTELLIGENCE SUMMARY

(Erase heading not required.)

Army Form C. 2118

Place	Date	Hour	Summary of Events and Information	Remarks and references to Appendices
LESTREM	4.3.16		Routine work. Sanitary during most of the day.	
"	5.3.16		Arranged with A.D.V.S. 38th Div. to take over his M.V.S billet at PARADIS.	
"	6.3.16		Visited Mobile Veterinary Section. Inspected horses for evacuation. 105 P. Ambulance and ordered two H.D. to be evacuated. A full of convoy during the day.	
"	7.3.16	10 am	Visited Mobile Veterinary Section.	
		11 am	Inspected two sick horses with No. 1 C.A.T.C. 35th Division horses. Ordered two of anyone to him + one of Lammelis; arranged for these to be evacuated. One case of anyone during the day.	
"	8.3.16	11 p.m	Inspected A.5th Mobile Veterinary Section in new area Q.12. Inspected all V.Cs of Division to attend a conference at M.V.S. Inspected 2 horses at ST. FLORIS (35 Div. horses) case for evacuation.	

WAR DIARY or INTELLIGENCE SUMMARY

Army Form C. 2118

Place	Date	Hour	Summary of Events and Information	Remarks and references to Appendices
LESTREM	9.3.16		Inspected 107th Field Ambulance. Horses in the open on hard standings. Condition & health good. Evacuated a mare in foal. Weather frosty.	
"	10.3.16		Inspected No. 2 & 3 Sections 35th Divisional Ammunition Column. Mules in fair condition; sent two mules to M.V.S. for evacuation. No. 2 Section horse lines on a sink road. Instructed O.C. No. 3 Section to evacuate 3 horses for debility.	
		3.P.M.	Conference of V.Os of Division at the Mobile Veterinary Section. Instructed V.Os to test all horses and those showing acute mallein hypersensitive reaction method. A.V.C. clerks report for duty.	
		6 PM	Wired D.H.Q. to send two men from Gloucester on arrival of draining at ABBEVILLE.	

WAR DIARY
or
INTELLIGENCE SUMMARY
(Erase heading not required.)

Army Form C. 2118

Instructions regarding War Diaries and Intelligence Summaries are contained in F. S. Regs., Part II. and the Staff Manual respectively. Title Pages will be prepared in manuscript.

Place	Date	Hour	Summary of Events and Information	Remarks and references to Appendices
LESTREM	11.3.16	11 am	Inspected Amm. Col. of 150th Bde. R.F.A.: animals in fair condition; health good; lines very muddy. Advised removal of lines if possible. Inspected C. Battery 158th Bty. R.F.A: Animals in fair condition; lines on hard standings; poor ventilation for one horse to be remedied. Impure horses being evacuated by 45th M.V.S. at MERVILLE STN. Weather milder.	
"	12.3.16		Medical Return & made to 35th Depot Co.: Into week pub febd outbred. " " " " D.A.D.Q.	
		4 PM	Inspected over A.B. horses in No. 2. A.T.C. & ordered its evacuation. horses in D Battery 163rd Bty. R.F.A. reported with discharge from one nostril; probably due to a kick on muzzle been when attack is a recent; tested the animal with mallein. Weather milder.	

WAR DIARY
or
INTELLIGENCE SUMMARY

(Erase heading not required.)

Army Form C. 2118

Instructions regarding War Diaries and Intelligence Summaries are contained in F. S. Regs, Part II. and the Staff Manual respectively. Title Pages will be prepared in manuscript.

Place	Date	Hour	Summary of Events and Information	Remarks and references to Appendices
LESTREM	13.3.16	10.30	Proceeded to PARADIS to inspect 1.5th M.V.S. with D.D.V.S. 1st Army.	
		3 P.M.	Inspected D Battery 163rd Brigade R.F.A. Animals in good condition. Ammunition Echelon of 163rd Brigade R.F.A. Some animals in light condition, especially those that have been clipped; recommended that these should be kept together & have extra feed and shelter if possible. Impartial Horses of Signal Co. & D.H.Q. that have been mobilised; no reactions.	
"	14.3.16	5.30	Inspected No. 4 Co. A.T.C.: Horses on hard standings; condition & health good. 106th Infantry Bde: Animals mostly under shelter; condition good.	
		3 P.M.	Ammunition Echelon of 157th F.A. Bde.: Animals picketted in an orchard; condition fair; health good.	
		4 P.M.	45th Mobile Veterinary Section & Horses for examination.	

WAR DIARY or INTELLIGENCE SUMMARY

Army Form C. 2118

(6)

Place	Date	Hour	Summary of Events and Information	Remarks and references to Appendices
LESTREM	15.3.16	10 am	Inspected animals of Pioneer Bn; condition & health good; animals under tent. Evacuated one car to N.V.I. Inspected 203rd & 204th F.C. R.E. Animals in the open on hard standings; condition & health good. Inspected one horse of 203rd F.C. R.E. with a kick causing injury to elbow and ordered its destruction.	
"	16.3.16	10 am	Inspected A + B batteries 158th F.A. Bgy. Animals in open on hard standings; condition good; health good. " N.1.C. N.T.C. Animals under open shelters; condition & health good. " 15th Cheshires (10.5th Bde) Animals picketed in the open; condition & health good. One Mule ordered to be evacuated.	

Army Form C. 2118

WAR DIARY
or
INTELLIGENCE SUMMARY
(Erase heading not required.)

Instructions regarding War Diaries and Intelligence Summaries are contained in F. S. Regs., Part II. and the Staff Manual respectively. Title Pages will be prepared in manuscript.

Place	Date	Hour	Summary of Events and Information	Remarks and references to Appendices
LESTREM	17.3.16	9.30	Inspected over horses Howser Bty. & evacuated at. to the M.V.I.	
"		10 am	C Battery 157th Bde. R.F.A.; Condition fair; a number of horses in light condition	
"		3 pm	Conference of V.Os at Mobile Veterinary Section.	
"	18.3.16	9.30	Inspected A,B,C & D batteries 159th Bde. R.F.A. Horses in very good condition & considered normal.	
"			A. Bty 163rd Howst. Bty. Horses in rather light condition.	
"			A,B, & D Batteries 157th Bde. R.F.A. at number of horses are in light condition, and do not compare with 159th F.A. Bde.; Reported the matter to D.A.D.	
"		4 pm	Inspected 1 H.D. horse accidentally shot by a man of the D.T.S., instructed them to return the horses for a few days.	

1875 Wt. W 593/826 1,000,000 4/15 J.B.C. & A. A.D.S.S./Forms/C. 2118.

Army Form C. 2118

G81

WAR DIARY
or
INTELLIGENCE SUMMARY
(Erase heading not required.)

Instructions regarding War Diaries and Intelligence Summaries are contained in F. S. Regs., Part II. and the Staff Manual respectively. Title Pages will be prepared in manuscript.

Place	Date	Hour	Summary of Events and Information	Remarks and references to Appendices
LESTREM	19.3.16	10 am	Inspected Ammunition Column of 159th F.A. Bde.: Horses in fair condition; what is improving; condition not so good as battery horses.	
		2.30 pm	" C Battery 163rd How. Bty. Condition of horses good.	
		4 pm	Visited Mobile Veterinary Section. Weather warm + dry: ground drying rapidly.	
"	20.3.16	11 am	Inspected No 1 + 3 Sections D.A.C. Mules in good condition; some horses in No.1 Section in bad condition. Horses in fair condition; some horses to M.V.S. Evacuated 2 horses to M.V.S.	
"	21.3.16	11 am	Inspected Ammunition Column of 163rd Brigade Bde.: Animals in fair condition: health good + condition improving.	
"	22.3.16		Visited Mobile Veterinary Section + inspected horses for evacuation.	

(91)

Army Form C. 2118

Instructions regarding War Diaries and Intelligence Summaries are contained in F.S. Regs., Part II. and the Staff Manual respectively. Title Pages will be prepared in manuscript.

WAR DIARY
or
INTELLIGENCE SUMMARY
(Erase heading not required.)

Place	Date	Hour	Summary of Events and Information	Remarks and references to Appendices
LESTREM.	23.3.16	10 am	Called on A.D.V.S. 8"Div. with a view to taking over the M.V.S. billet in his area on movement of the Division.	
"		4 P.M	Inspected 2 horses from No 3 C.A.V.C. (chronic laminitis) to M.V.S.	
"	24.3.16	3 P.M	Conference of V.Os at Mobile Veterinary Section. The causes of colic & laminitis were discussed.	
"	25.3.16		Inspected horses for evacuation to base	
"	26.3.16		Units moving into a new area.	
"	27.3.16		Units moving into a new area.	
"	28.3.16	11 am	Change of D.H.Q. to SAILLY-SUR-LYS. Inspected 107th F. Ambulance. Horses in fair condition.	
SAILLY	29.3.16		Inspected Mobile Veterinary Section at new position. Position & accommodation good.	

Army Form C. 2118

WAR DIARY
or
INTELLIGENCE SUMMARY
(Erase heading not required.)

Instructions regarding War Diaries and Intelligence Summaries are contained in F. S. Regs., Part II. and the Staff Manual respectively. Title Pages will be prepared in manuscript.

Place	Date	Hour	Summary of Events and Information	Remarks and references to Appendices
SAILLY	30.3.16		Inspected 104th Infantry Bde. Animals in fair condition & health good.	
			" 181st Mining Co: Strength 11 horses; condition good.	
		3 P.M.	Conference of V.G. at M.V.T.	
" "	31.3.16		Inspection of 106th Infantry Bde. Animals in good condition. Shoeing of though had to needs improvement.	
			" 205th F. C. R.E. Animals in good condition.	

1875 Wt. W593/826 1,000,000 4/15 I B.C. & A. A.D.S.S./Forms/C. 2118.

Army Form C. 2118

ADVS

WAR DIARY of A.D.V.S. 35th Division.

or

INTELLIGENCE SUMMARY

(Erase heading not required.)

Instructions regarding War Diaries and Intelligence Summaries are contained in F. S. Regs., Part II. and the Staff Manual respectively. Title Pages will be prepared in manuscript.

Place	Date	Hour	Summary of Events and Information	Remarks and references to Appendices
SAILLY	1.4.16		Visited Mobile Veterinary Section. Weather poor.	35T VM 3
"	2.4.16		Inspected 105" Infantry Brigade. Animals under shelter; condition fair; Thirty of 15" Cheshires indifferent. 204" Field Co. R.E. " Horses on hard standings in the open; condition fair; health good.	
"	3.4.16		Inspected 35" D.A.C. No 1 Section in the open; condition fair. " 2 " 50% under shelter " " " 3 " in the open " " Few casualties.	
"	4.4.16		Inspected 168" Infantry Brigade with O.C. Brigade. C. & D. Batteries in good condition. A. Battery: horses picketed in two lines somewhat; attention of O.C. Brigade brought to this matter. B. Battery: condition fair; regs. horses hyped. Ammn Col. " " ; own horses in hyped condition.	

1875 Wt. W503/826. 1,000,000. 4/15 T.R.C. & A. A.D.S.S./Forms/C.2118.

(2)

Army Form C. 2118

Instructions regarding War Diaries and Intelligence Summaries are contained in F. S. Regs., Part II. and the Staff Manual respectively. Title Pages will be prepared in manuscript.

WAR DIARY
or
INTELLIGENCE SUMMARY
(Erase heading not required.)

Place	Date	Hour	Summary of Events and Information	Remarks and references to Appendices
SAILLY	4.4.16	3 pm	Inspected 110" H. By. R.G.A. & "B" Brigade. Horses in very good condition; health good; inoculated men to T.V.I.	
" "	5.4.16		C.R.A. 35th Division reports that Lieut. Langmore A.V.C. attached to 163rd Howitzer Brigade is placed under arrest by order of the Corps Commander for conduct to the prejudice of good order and military discipline; A summary of evidence is being taken by order of O.C. 163rd Bde. R.F.A.	
		10 am	Inspected 109" H. By. R.G.A. Horses in good condition; Northumberland Fusiliers two companies. Animals in very good condition.	
		1 pm.	203" F. C. R.E. Condition & health of animals good.	
" "	6.4.16		Inspected 35th Div. Imperial Co. Animals generally in good condition; Took over Veterinary administration of 4 "Kemmey Brigade".	

(3)

Army Form C. 2118

WAR DIARY
or
INTELLIGENCE SUMMARY
(Erase heading not required.)

Instructions regarding War Diaries and Intelligence Summaries are contained in F. S. Regs., Part II. and the Staff Manual respectively. Title Pages will be prepared in manuscript.

Place	Date	Hour	Summary of Events and Information	Remarks and references to Appendices
SAILLY.	7/4/16		Inspected 35th Divisional Train. Horses on Nos 2 & 3 lines in light condition. Health good. Condition generally good.	
" "	8/4/16		Inspected 118, 186 & 5/5 R.G.A. 4" Heavy Howitzers. Condition of horses fair; too many prancing buck and tentenant not making quite fit team. Recommended Borax oral & Chlorate of Potass in treatment. Inspected Warwickshire Battery R.G.A. & Div. Ammunition Park. Horses in fair condition, a few horses in too light condition.	
" "	9/4/16.		Inspected 35th Divisional Cavalry. Animals in good condition & few casualties. 106" & Ambulance Animals in good condition.	
" "	10/4/16 10 am		Received report from C.R.A. 35 Division that 2 Lieut f. M-- team attacked near yesterday. Placed under arrest by the A.P.M. for drunkenness. Inspected all sick animals of 4" Heavy Howitzers Brigade.	159 F.A.V.C.

Army Form C. 2118

WAR DIARY
or
INTELLIGENCE SUMMARY
(Erase heading not required.)

Instructions regarding War Diaries and Intelligence Summaries are contained in F. S. Regs., Part II. and the Staff Manual respectively. Title Pages will be prepared in manuscript.

Place	Date	Hour	Summary of Events and Information	Remarks and references to Appendices
SAILLY.	11.4.16		Inspected detachment horses of 110th N. Bty. R.G.A. belonging to observation party. Met Lieut. Turner A.V.C. at LA GORGUE & took him to his unit.	
"	12.4.16		Inspected sick horses of 4th Heavy Bde. Evacuated 3 cases to M.V.S. " horses of 205th F.C. R.E. Animals in good condition.	
		3 P.M.	Visited M.V.S.	
"	13.4.16		Inspected horses of A,B,C & D Batteries 150th The R.F.A. A & B in fair condition: condition improved. C & D some horses still in bad condition. Grooming insufficient: health generally good & not many casualties.	
"	14.4.16	5 P.M.	Conference of V.Os at Mobile Veterinary Section.	
"	15.4.16		Routine work.	
"	16.4.16	3 P.M.	Conference at H.Q. 1st Army.	

1875 Wt. W593/826 1,000,000 4/15 I.P.C. & A. A.D.S.S./Forms/C. 2118.

Army Form C. 2118

(5)

Instructions regarding War Diaries and Intelligence Summaries are contained in F. S. Regs., Part II. and the Staff Manual respectively. Title Pages will be prepared in manuscript.

WAR DIARY
or
INTELLIGENCE SUMMARY
(Erase heading not required.)

Place	Date	Hour	Summary of Events and Information	Remarks and references to Appendices
SAILLY	17.4.16		Inspected Pharaoh Mr. Animals in good condition.	
"			205th F.C. R.E. Animals in good condition; some rabbles.	
"	18.4.16		Routine work: weather wet. Units moving into new areas.	
"	19.4.16	3 pm	Visited Mobile Veterinary Section. Units moving into new area.	
"	20.4.16	10 am	Change of D.H.Q. to LESTREM. Inspected Brigade Ammn. Col. of 158th Bde R.F.A. Horses in fair condition; proving indifferent.	
"		3 pm	Called on A.D.V.S. 39th Div. re Corps troops in new area. Conference & K.G. at Mobile Veterinary Section.	
LESTREM	21.4.16	3 pm		
"	22.4.16		Inspected C. Battery 159 F.A. Bde. Horses in good condition & fair condition.	
"			203rd F.C. R.E. condition of animals good.	
"			1 Co. Northumberland Fusiliers. Animals in poor condition. Lieut Simpson A.V.C. left for No 6 V.H. at ROUEN.	

WAR DIARY or INTELLIGENCE SUMMARY

Army Form C. 2118

Place	Date	Hour	Summary of Events and Information	Remarks and references to Appendices
LESTREM	23.4.16	10 am	Inspected No. 1 C. 35" Div. Amm. Col. Ammn. in good condition. Some horses returned from attachment to Divisional Amm. Col. not in good condition, but somewhat sight. Inspected No. 2 C. 35" Div. Amm. Col. Ammn. in fair condition. Rehorsed in the open.	
"	24.4.16	10 am	Inspected 157 F.A. Bde. A. Battery condition fair. B " " " C " " " D " " " Adm. Col " " " Condition has improved, few casualties, growing intelligent. Inspected No. 3 C. 35" Div. Amm. Col. Condition fair: machinery arrangement to load: Animals C.C. to work from a trough.	
"	25.4.16		Inspected A B & D Batteries 159" Bde. R.F.A. Horses passed in good condition: Casualties normal.	

WAR DIARY or INTELLIGENCE SUMMARY

Army Form C. 2118

Place	Date	Hour	Summary of Events and Information	Remarks and references to Appendices
LESTREM	26.4.16		Inspected 35" Heavy Battery. Horses in fair condition; casualties normal.	
"	27.4.16		Inspected 35" Trench M. R.B. Animals in fair condition.	
"		6.30 PM	C.R.A. interviewed Lieut. McLean & relieved him from arrest.	
"	28.4.16		Inspected A.C. & D. Batteries 163rd Bde R.F.A. with O.C. Brigade. A Battery; animals in fair condition, some horses too light, improving; indifferent. C & D Batteries in good condition.	
"		3 PM	Conference of V.Os at M.V.T.	
"	29.4.16		Issued orders to Lieut. Pitakeye to proceed to No. 14 Veterinary Hospital at ABBEVILLE.	
"	30.4.16		Lieut. R Pitakeye M.V.C. proceeded on transfer to No. 14 Veterinary Hospital, ABBEVILLE. N. & Lowe ." reported himself for duty with 35th Divn.	

WN Taylor
Major AVC
35 Divn

1.5.16

WAR DIARY of A.D.V.S. 35th Div.

INTELLIGENCE SUMMARY
(Erase heading not required.)

Army Form C. 2118

Place	Date	Hour	Summary of Events and Information	Remarks and references to Appendices
LESTREM	1.5.16		Inspected 20th Divisional Sanitaires. " D.T.B. 18th " " D.T.B. " " F.T.B. " " West Yorks " Arrived in good condition with few casualties.	
"	2.5.16		Arranged for inspection of all units of Division of D.D.V.S. 1st Army. Programme started & conducted.	1 attached
"	3.5.16		D.D.V.S. 1st Army inspected the following:— 35th D.A.C. ; 163rd Bde R.F.A. ; 106th Infantry Bde & M.G. Coy. ; 35th Div Train	
"	4.5.16		D.D.V.S. " inspected 105, 106 & 107 F. Ambulances 35th Div Cavalry Sqn. 105th Infantry Bde & Pioneer Bn. 203rd, 204 & 205 F. Coys R.E. D. Battery 163rd F.A. Bde.	
"	5.5.16		D.D.V.S. 1st Army inspected the following units:— 157, 158 & 159 F. A. Bdes. 104th Bde Units & M.G. Coy.	2 attached

(2) Army Form C. 2118

WAR DIARY or INTELLIGENCE SUMMARY

(Erase heading not required.)

Instructions regarding War Diaries and Intelligence Summaries are contained in F. S. Regs., Part II and the Staff Manual respectively. Title Pages will be prepared in manuscript.

Place	Date	Hour	Summary of Events and Information	Remarks and references to Appendices
LESTREM	6.5.16	10 am	Inspected horses at 45" M.V.1. for evacuation.	
"	7.5.16	3 p.m.	Attended Conference of A.D.V.1 at 1st Army.	
"	8.5.16	10 am	Visited M.V.1.	
"	9.5.16		O.C. 45" M.V.A. proceeded on leave to England, also to attend investiture on 10" inst. took over charge of M.V.1.	
"	10.5.16		Inspected the remounts at LA GORGUE.	
"	11.5.16		Inspected M.G. Squadron horses. Horses in a misical lot; condition good. Unit leaving the Div. on Saturday next.	
"	12.5.16		Conference of V.Os of Division at M.V.1.	
"	13.5.16		Inspected 26 ordinary cases for evacuation to Base	
"	14.5.16		Pancutin.	
"	15.5.16		Inspected B. battery 158" Bde R.F.A. Horses in fair condition.	

1875 Wt. W593/826 1,000,000 4/15 J.B.C. & A. A.D.S.S./Forms/C. 2118.

WAR DIARY or INTELLIGENCE SUMMARY

Army Form C. 2118

(Erase heading not required.)

Instructions regarding War Diaries and Intelligence Summaries are contained in F.S. Regs., Part II. and the Staff Manual respectively. Title Pages will be prepared in manuscript.

Place	Date	Hour	Summary of Events and Information	Remarks and references to Appendices
LESTREM	16.5.16		Inspected 107" F. Ambulance. Animals in good condition. B.W.C. 157th Bde R.F.A. Condition of animals good.	
"	17.5.16		Inspected B.W.C. 158th Bde R.F.A. Horses in fair condition. One horse of 15" Howitzer evacuated to M.V.S.	
"	18.5.16		20th Divisional Sanitaire. Horses & mules generally in good condition. M.G. Coy 105" Infantry Bde. Shoeing bad; feet long; animals in fair condition. 105" F. Ambulance. Horses in poor condition; inadequate veterinary chest & Wallets. 105" " " Horses in poor condition. 106" " " Horses in good condition.	
"	19.5.16		Conference of V.Gs at M.V.S. N.C.O. on horse that had from showing symptoms of strychnine. An abscess was formed containing the oesophagus at the entrance of chest between the two exits, & probably opened on gullet.	
"	20.5.16		Examined on post-mortem two horses of the 158" B.A.C. that from assault & symptoms related indicated that cause was common vegetable poisoning. Viscera were retained showing great prostration with chloral purish. Report sent to D.N.Q. with sample of oat containing a large percentage of common vetch.	

1875 Wt. W593/826 1,000,000 4/15 J.B.C. & A. A.D.S.S./Forms/C. 2118.

Army Form C. 2118

WAR DIARY
or
INTELLIGENCE SUMMARY
(Erase heading not required.)

Instructions regarding War Diaries and Intelligence Summaries are contained in F.S. Regs., Part II. and the Staff Manual respectively. Title Pages will be prepared in manuscript.

Place	Date	Hour	Summary of Events and Information	Remarks and references to Appendices
LESTREM	21.5.16	10 am	Inspected on foot-motion and A.D. horse; nothing definite to report. Dummy showed abnormal symptom of great prostration, disturbed peristalsis, may have food poisoning. Temp. 103°F. No other case in stag mart. 106. F. Ambulances. On the cars on their march to the horses & the 150 B.W.C., and these had greatly improved. Inspected G.C.O.N.C. reference arrangements & D.W.C., & inspection of another horses before departure.	
"	22.5.16	10 am	Interviewed G.C.O.N.C. reference arrangements & D.W.C., & inspection of another horses before departure.	
"	23.5.16		Routine. D.D.V.S. called at office.	
"	24.5.16		Inspected V.G. Pioneer Bn: Animals in good condition: Shoeing fair. " 20th Field Co. R.E: " " good condition: " " good.	
"	25.5.16		Inspected another command after reorganisation to D.V.A.C. Sent 17 horses & 2 mules to M.V.1 for evacuation.	
"	26.5.16		Inspected West Yorks Bn: Shoeing fair; animals in good condition; some feet still long. Animals in good condition: " D.T.T. & N.T.T.! Animals in good condition & shoeing fair which has improved. " 104th Fd. M.S.Co " " shoeing backbone feet long. " 203rd F.C. R.E. Animals in good condition; shoeing fair; some mules feet still too long.
		3 pm	Conference K.V.Os at M.V.1/1.	

1875 Wt. W593/826 1,000,000 4/15 J.B.C. & A. A.D.S.S./Forms/C. 2118.

WAR DIARY
or
INTELLIGENCE SUMMARY

Army Form C. 2118

Place	Date	Hour	Summary of Events and Information	Remarks and references to Appendices
LESTREM	27.5.16		Inspected 9" Lowndes Howitzer: Muzzle on light side; showing burst. Proven in good condition. Inspected the transport Officer, that ammunition should be inserted from a triangle and not from common funnel 5. Inspected 18" Ammunition Limbers: Ammunition in good condition; showing fair. One made with Platoon to be sent of Fleet to M.T.O. Chapel Carts; harness & needles in good condition; showing fair.	
"	28.5.16		Inspected No. 3 & 4 Co. A.S.C. Ammunition in good condition; showing good.	
"	29.5.16		Inspected 105" Light Police. Ammunition in good condition; showing fair uniformed. 105" Infy. Bde. M.S. Co. Ammunition in fair condition; showing breakwork.	
"	30.5.16		Inspected 205" P. Co. R.E. Ammunition in good condition; also intact Verbenay Knapes & fuzed at on good exposition. " C. 86, 159" & A. Bde. " " " 106" M.S. Co. Ammunition in fair condition; showing breakwork. " 106 Bde. M. Gun horses; " "	

Army Form C. 2118

WAR DIARY
or
INTELLIGENCE SUMMARY
(Erase heading not required.)

Place	Date	Hour	Summary of Events and Information	Remarks and references to Appendices
LESTREM	31.5.16		Inspected 163rd Bde R.F.A. Animals in good condition; showing fair ; cumulative fever.	

W R Taylor 1.6.16
Major A.V.C.
A.D.V.S. 35 Div
(1916)

A.D.V.S.

Appendix I

35 D/1459/A.

The D.D.V.S. First Army will inspect the horses and mules of units as follows :-

Wednesday 3rd May.

D.A.C. PARADIS at Q.18.a.4.7. at 10.30 a.m.

163rd Bde R.F.A. & B.A.C. at EPINETTE R.13.d.4.9. 11-30 a.m.

106th Bde Units; M.G. Coy. incl. at CROIX MARMUSE R.20.a.4.4. 2-15 p.m.

35th Div. Train at R.8.d.8.1. 3.15 p.m.

Thursday 4th May. 12.15 PM

105th, 106th & 107th Fd.Ambce at ZELOBES R.26.d.9.3. at 10.30 am.

35th Div. Cavalry, near Church PARADIS 11-30 a.m.

105th Bde Units at X.3.d. central.)
203rd, 204th & 205th Fd.Cos. R.E. ") 2. 15 p.m.
35th Div Pioneers. ")

35th Div. Signal Coy. at LESTREM. 3. 30. p.m.

Friday 5th May.

157th F.A. Bde & B.A.C. LES LOBES R.32.d.1.3. 10. 30 a.m.

158th " " " CROIX MARMUSE R.20.c.5.9. 11.30 a.m.

104th Bde Units: M.G. Coy. incl. FOSSE. R.22.a.5.5. 2.15 p.m.

159th F.A. Bde & B.A.C. ZELOBES R.26.d.6.9. at 3 p.m.

One man to two horses will be enough of the personnel.

D.H.Q.
2. 5. 16.

A. HASTED. Lt. Col.
A.A. & Q.M.G.
35th Division.

Army Form C. 2118

WAR DIARY of **A.D.V.S. 35th Div.**
or
INTELLIGENCE SUMMARY
(Erase heading not required.)

Vol 5

Place	Date	Hour	Summary of Events and Information	Remarks and references to Appendices
LESTREM	1.6.16		Inspected 159 Bde. R.F.A. Animals in good condition; shoeing fair.	
"	2.6.16		Inspected C Bty 157 Bde R.F.A. Animals in good condition; shoeing fair.	
			D " 157 Bde R.F.A. Animals in good condition; require more grooming.	
			C 155 157 Bde R.F.A. Animals in good condition.	
			A/c V.60 at M.V.S.	
"	3.6.16	3.pm	Conference of Nos 1, 2, 3 sections D.A.C. Horses in good condition; casualties normal.	
"	4.6.16	10 am	Inspected M.H. Section D.A.C. Mules in good condition; shoeing of some mules not neglected.	
"		3.pm	Conference of A.D.V.S at 1st Army H.Q.	

Army Form C. 2118

WAR DIARY
or
INTELLIGENCE SUMMARY
(Erase heading not required.)

(A) i

Instructions regarding War Diaries and Intelligence Summaries are contained in F. S. Regs., Part II. and the Staff Manual respectively. Title Pages will be prepared in manuscript.

Place	Date	Hour	Summary of Events and Information	Remarks and references to Appendices
LESTREM	5.6.16	10 am	Reported A Battery 157th F.A. Bde. then battery has just returned from training area. Arrivals in fair good condition; a few horses in slight arde. Shoeing fair.	
" "	6.6.16		Reported 104th Infantry Bde. M.G.Co.; as to shoeing. Shoeing & mules improving.	
" "	7.6.16	10 am	Reported B. Battery 159th F.A. Bde. Condition of horses good. " " 157th F.A. Bde. Condition of horses good; a few horses in slight condition. B Battery 158th F.A. Bde. Condition of horses good.	
" "	8.6.16		Reported No. 1 & 2 Cos. A.A.C. Animals in fair condition but too many slight casualties.	
" "	9.6.16	3 p.m.	Inspected V.Gs at M.V.? Inspection of sick horses for evacuation.	

Army Form C. 2118

WAR DIARY
or
INTELLIGENCE SUMMARY
(Erase heading not required.)

Instructions regarding War Diaries and Intelligence Summaries are contained in F. S. Regs., Part II and the Staff Manual respectively. Title Pages will be prepared in manuscript.

Place	Date	Hour	Summary of Events and Information	Remarks and references to Appendices
ESTREM	10.6.16	12 Noon	Inspected sick horses entrained at Pontluent.	
"	11.6.16	5 p.m.	Inspected all A.V.C. Sergeants of Division in Mounting Order, at Mobile Veterinary Section. Sergeants attached to D.A.V.C. army in-Infantry, but all M.C.G. were well turned out. Webb's in good condition.	
"	12.6.16	10 am	Inspected No 4 Section 1st Portions Park (Army Troops) two N.I.D. horses with skin eruption of suspected mange were sent to M.V.1 for full examination & observation. Arranged for all horses to be dressed with Calcium Sulphide & other preventive measures.	
"	13.6.16		Routine work. Lieut J.F. Park A.V.C. proceed on 7 days leave to England.	
"	14.6.16		Routine work. Weather damp & cold. Visited A.O. Vet. 61st Division.	
"	15.6.16		Inspected horses at M.V.1 for evacuation to Rouen.	
"	16.6.16		Conference of V.Os at M.V.1.	
"	17.6.16		Proceed to new Head quarters at BUSNES.	

Army Form C. 2118

WAR DIARY
or
INTELLIGENCE SUMMARY
(Erase heading not required.)

Instructions regarding War Diaries and Intelligence Summaries are contained in F. S. Regs., Part II. and the Staff Manual respectively. Title Pages will be prepared in manuscript.

Place	Date	Hour	Summary of Events and Information	Remarks and references to Appendices
BUSNES	18.6.16.		Called at R.A. Hdt 2tn re Artillery Inurnoning in East area. Visited M.V.I in our area.	
"	19.6.16.		Sunday.	
"	20.6.16		Inspected M.V.G. M.T.C. Horses in good condition. 203", 202" & 205" F.Coy R.E. Condition of animals good.	
"	21.6.16		Inspected No 2 + Coy A.T.C. Condition of animals good. 17", 20 + 18" Lancashire Fusiliers :- Animals in good condition. Sharing of 20" Lancashire Fusiliers Mules & horses not good. Inspected 10", 11th Batt 25, & Bomb. transport animals being fed off the ground. 12 Batt: 25 to Staff/6 Captains: Condition of animals good. Inspected 10.6" F. Ambulance : condition of animals good.	

1875 Wt. W593/826 1,000,000 4/15 J.B.C. & A. A.D.S.S./Forms/C. 2118.

Army Form C. 2118

WAR DIARY
or
INTELLIGENCE SUMMARY
(Erase heading not required.)

Instructions regarding War Diaries and Intelligence Summaries are contained in F. S. Regs., Part II. and the Staff Manual respectively. Title Pages will be prepared in manuscript.

Place	Date	Hour	Summary of Events and Information	Remarks and references to Appendices
BOSMES	22.6.16		Inspected Reserve M/n; Ammunition in good condition; Showing first Indication of need to N.V.R.	
" "	23.6.16		Inspected the 4.5" Mobile Veterinary Section in coming order.	
			" " the " " small trunks out.	
			" " with harness for ammunition.	
" "	24.6.16		Routine.	
" "	25.6.16		Inspected 'A' Battery 157" 126 R.F.A. Ammunition in fair condition.	
" "	26.6.16		Inspected A. 168 126 R.F.A. Ammunition in good condition; ammunition normal.	
			" " D 159 & C. 157 126 R.F.A.; Ammunition in fair condition.	
			" " C. 158 126 R.F.A. Ammunition in good condition.	
			" " C. 15.9 126 R.F.A. Ammunition in very good condition.	
" "	27.6.16		Routine.	

Army Form C. 2118

WAR DIARY
or
INTELLIGENCE SUMMARY
(Erase heading not required.)

Instructions regarding War Diaries and Intelligence Summaries are contained in F. S. Regs., Part II. and the Staff Manual respectively. Title Pages will be prepared in manuscript.

Place	Date	Hour	Summary of Events and Information	Remarks and references to Appendices
BUSNES.	28.6.16		Rendezvous O.C. M.V.S. to forward to B.R.V.A.S. with the rendezvous on 29.6.16.	
"	29.6.16.		Rendezvous.	
"	30.6.16		Rendezvous 45th M.V.S. in new area.	

W.N. Laughn Major A.V.C.
A.D.V.S. 35th Div.

WAR DIARY of A.D.V.S. 35th Divn

July

Vol 6

INTELLIGENCE SUMMARY

(Erase heading not required.)

Place	Date	Hour	Summary of Events and Information	Remarks and references to Appendices
BUSNES	1.7.16		Inspection of sick horses for evacuation by the Mobile Veterinary Section.	
"	2.7.16		Proceeded to BOUELENS.	
BOUELENS	3.7.16		Inspected horses of 35th Hospital Co. Condition & shoeing generally good.	
"	4.7.16		Inspected Mobile Veterinary Section in new area.	
			" Horses of 106" Field Ambulance; condition generally good.	
			" ammunition of 19" Northumberland Fusiliers Condition of ammunition good.	
			" B Battery Division 165" F.A. Bde. Condition & shoeing generally good.	
"	5.7.16		Mobile Veterinary Section proceeded to GEZAINCOURT in Artillery area.	
"	6.7.16		Inspected sick horses at Mobile Veterinary Station for evacuation to Hospital.	

(2)

Army Form C. 2118

WAR DIARY
or
INTELLIGENCE SUMMARY
(Erase heading not required.)

Instructions regarding War Diaries and Intelligence Summaries are contained in F.S. Regs., Part II. and the Staff Manual respectively. Title Pages will be prepared in manuscript.

Place	Date	Hour	Summary of Events and Information	Remarks and references to Appendices
DOULLENS	7.7.16		Proceeded to BUS-LES-ARTOIS in charge of D.N.Q.	
BUS-LES-ARTOIS	8.7.16		Inspected Mobile Veterinary Section in new accommodation and horses interned at BOUQUEMAISON.	
"	9.7.16		Inspected horses of 106th Infantry Brigade. Four amount were sick to Veterinary Section. Conducted to command post.	
CONTAY	10.7.16		Proceeded to CONTAY in charge of D.N.Q.	
"	11.7.16		Inspected sick horses with Mobile Section for evacuation to hospital. Arranged for MVS to proceed to LEALVILLERS.	
"	12.7.16		Inspected horses of 1st, 2nd, 3rd & 4th Bns. 95th Divn. Found animals in good condition. Three mules received severe contusions to the feet having dumped in during return journey and to O.C.	

1875 Wt. W593/826 1,000,000 4/15 J.B.C. & A. A.D.S.S./Forms/C. 2118.

Army Form C. 2118

WAR DIARY
or
INTELLIGENCE SUMMARY
(Erase heading not required.)

(3)

Instructions regarding War Diaries and Intelligence Summaries are contained in F.S. Regs., Part II. and the Staff Manual respectively. Title Pages will be prepared in manuscript.

Place	Date	Hour	Summary of Events and Information	Remarks and references to Appendices
MORLANCOURT	13.7.16		Proceeded to MORLANCOURT. Received 1 Mule belonging to 7th Divn. M.V.A.	
"	14.7.16		Arranged for Mobile Veterinary Section to live at MORLANCOURT.	
"	15.7.16		Rendezvous with horses at LEAVILLERS for evacuation to BASE.	
"	16.7.16		Inspected 104th Bde Pack Unit. Animals in good condition. Some 15 M.G. Co. mules in light condition, showing indifferent " 105th Bde animals. Animals in good condition. M.G. Co. mules have condition; chasing poor. Ammunition Advanced collecting post at BRONFAY FME.	

1875 Wt. W593/826 1,000,000 4/15 J.B.C. & A. A.D.S.S./Forms/C. 2118.

(4)

Army Form C. 2118

WAR DIARY
or
INTELLIGENCE SUMMARY
(Erase heading not required.)

Instructions regarding War Diaries and Intelligence Summaries are contained in F. S. Regs., Part II. and the Staff Manual respectively. Title Pages will be prepared in manuscript.

Place	Date	Hour	Summary of Events and Information	Remarks and references to Appendices
MORLANCOURT	17/7/16		Inspected sick horses for evacuation to Base hospital.	
"	18/7/16		Inspected 106° Fd. Unit at CARNOY VALLEY. Exhibits of animals good; some evacuation from shells.	
"	19/7/16		M/ Sergt. Rackham, A.V.C. att. 150° F.A. Bde reported sick.	
"	20/7/16		Inspected horses of Nos 1,2,3 & 4 Sec 35° Div Train. Condition & horses, general, good; few evacuations.	
"	21/7/16		Inspected 35° D.A.C. Horses in fair condition; shewing fair. Mules in good condition.	
"	22/7/16		Inspected horses of 107° F.A. Brigade. Condition & shewing, general.	
"	23/7/16		Inspected horses of 163rd F.A. Bde. Condition generally good, some horses in light condition; warm weather, starvation; long distances to water.	

(5)

Army Form C. 2118

Instructions regarding War Diaries and Intelligence
Summaries are contained in F. S. Regs., Part II.
and the Staff Manual respectively. Title Pages
will be prepared in manuscript.

WAR DIARY
or
INTELLIGENCE SUMMARY
(Erase heading not required.)

Place	Date	Hour	Summary of Events and Information	Remarks and references to Appendices
HARLANCOURT	24/7/16		Inspected sick horses for evacuation to hospital. Mostly chill amounts.	
"	25/7/16		Inspected horses of 159" F.A. Bde. Horses generally in good condition; work strenuous.	
"	26/7/16		Inspected horses of 157" F.A. Bde. Condition generally good, but some horses in slight condition; work strenuous.	
"	27/7/16		Inspected horses of 150" F.A. Bde. Condition generally good; work at present rather strenuous.	
"	28/7/16		Inspected sick horses for evacuation to hospital. Majority suffering from chills.	
"	29/7/16		Inspected horses of 35" Trench Co; condition good.	
"	30/7/16		sick horses for evacuation to hospital. Mostly chill amounts.	
"	31/7/16		107" F. Ambulance; Horses generally in good condition	

W.N. Taylor Major A.V.C.
A.D.V.S. 35 Div.

WAR DIARY A.D.V.1. 35th Division

INTELLIGENCE SUMMARY

(Erase heading not required.)

Army Form C. 2118.

Place	Date	Hour	Summary of Events and Information	Remarks and references to Appendices
MORLANCOURT	1.9.16		Inspected 105th Infantry Brigade front. Condition of 105th Bys. horses generally good. Shoeing fair. Shoeing of M.G.C. indifferent, but shows little improvement. 204th F. RE, condition & shoeing generally good. 106th F. Ambulance; one section; condition good.	
"	2.9.16		Inspected 106th Infantry Brigade front. Condition of 106th Bys. Bn. animals generally good; shoeing fair. Shoeing of M.G.Co indifferent; animals in fair condition. 205th F.C. R.E. – Condition & shoeing general good.	
"	3.9.16		Proceeded to GORBIE on change of D.H.Q. Lieut. J. McQueen A.V.C. (M.C.) proceeds to ENGLAND on termination of engagement.	

Army Form C. 2118.

WAR DIARY
or
INTELLIGENCE SUMMARY.
(Erase heading not required.)

Instructions regarding War Diaries and Intelligence Summaries are contained in F. S. Regs., Part II. and the Staff Manual respectively. Title pages will be prepared in manuscript.

Place	Date	Hour	Summary of Events and Information	Remarks and references to Appendices
MERLANCOURT	4.8.16		Mobile Veterinary Section moved to DAOURS.	
"	5.8.16		Proceeded to CAVILLON & change of D.H.Q. Mobile Veterinary Station moved to ST. PIERRE.	
		G.O.A.	Kinsler met at ST. PIERRE.	
CAVILLON	6.8.16		Reported horses of 35th Reg'al Co. & remounted over to M.V.A. Condition generally good.	
"	7.8.16		Inspected horses & mules of 104th Infantry Reln. Condition of animals generally good; shoeing fair.	
"	8.8.16		Inspected animals of 19th Motherland Fusiliers. Condition & shoeing good.	

WAR DIARY
or
INTELLIGENCE SUMMARY.
(Erase heading not required.)

Army Form C. 2118.

Place	Date	Hour	Summary of Events and Information	Remarks and references to Appendices
CAVILLON	9.9.16		Mobile Vet. Section entraining with horses & moves to DAOURS.	
CORBIE	10.9.16		Proceeded to CORBIE in charge of D.M.O.	
"	11.9.16		Mobile Vet. Section moves to MORLANCOURT.	
"	12.9.16		1 non. to Bn. Offr. umougst deputed on A. B.5 157th Fld. R.F.A. Reported Horses to D. anti-section & found no further cases. Vaccinary measures taken. Inspected M.V.S. at MORLANCOURT.	
"	13.9.16		M.M.P. horses evacuated to Mobile Veterinary Section with Sarcoptic mange. Precautionary measures taken.	

Army Form C. 2118.

WAR DIARY
or
INTELLIGENCE SUMMARY.
(Erase heading not required.)

Instructions regarding War Diaries and Intelligence Summaries are contained in F. S. Regs., Part II. and the Staff Manual respectively. Title pages will be prepared in manuscript.

Place	Date	Hour	Summary of Events and Information	Remarks and references to Appendices
CORBIE	14.9.16		Inspected horses of 150th F.A. Bde. A. Bty; condition fair; a number of horses in poor condition. B. & C. & D. Btys; condition fair.	
"	15.9.16		Proceeded to CITADEL with D.D.Q.	
CITADEL	16.9.16		Attended a conference of A.D.V.S., V.A. & Army at HERICOURT.	
"	17.9.16		Inspected horses of Maj. Paton D.V.O.C. Cavalry & Pioneer Lines. No 4 Section D.V.C. mules in good condition; showing of mules could improved.	
"	18.9.16		Inspected sick horses for evacuation at Mobile Veterinary Section.	

Army Form C. 2118.

WAR DIARY
or
INTELLIGENCE SUMMARY.
(Erase heading not required.)

Instructions regarding War Diaries and Intelligence Summaries are contained in F. S. Regs., Part II. and the Staff Manual respectively. Title pages will be prepared in manuscript.

Place	Date	Hour	Summary of Events and Information	Remarks and references to Appendices
CITADEL	19.9.16		Inspected 105", 106" & 107" F. Ambulances. Condition of command good; clothing fair.	
"	20.9.16		Inspected No 2 Section D.A.C. Condition of horses generally not good; some horses light; continued 6.6.; D.A.C. and arrangt. to give one of them a rest. Inspected 163rd Bde R.F.A. Condition of horses generally good; D Battery very good. C Btty, some horses in light condition.	
"	21.9.16		Inspected No. 3 Section D.A.C. Condition of horses fair.	
"	22.9.16		Inspected horses of Divisional Train; condition generally good; casualties normal.	
"	23.9.16		Inspected horses of 159th R.A. Bde at CORBIE. Condition & shoeing generally good.	

Army Form C. 2118.

WAR DIARY
or
INTELLIGENCE SUMMARY.
(Erase heading not required.)

Instructions regarding War Diaries and Intelligence Summaries are contained in F. S. Regs., Part II. and the Staff Manual respectively. Title pages will be prepared in manuscript.

Place	Date	Hour	Summary of Events and Information	Remarks and references to Appendices
CITADEL	24.8.16		Inspected 106th M.V.S.C.: condition of command good. Photog. still insufficient; men cannot overwork; furnished time out to Transport Officers, with a view to a remedy.	
	25.8.16		Weekly inspection of V.6. at Mobile Veterinary Section at MORLANCOURT.	
FORKED-TREE	26.8.16		D.N.9. moved to FORKED-TREE.	
"	27.8.16		Inspected horses & mules of Reserve Bde: condition good; shewing form	
"	28.8.16		Inspected sick horses at M.V.S. for evacuation to Base.	
"	29.8.16		Inspected sick horses at M.V.S. for evacuation to Hospital.	
DOULLENS	30.8.16		Moved to DOULLENS.	
"	31.8.16		Inspected horses of 35th Anzac L.C. condition good & few casualties on march.	

W.N. Taylor Major A.V.C.
A.D.V.S. 1 35 Div

T2134. Wt. W708—776. 500000. 4/15. Sir J. C. & S.

Army Form C. 2118.

VOL. 8

WAR DIARY M.V.1. 35th Div

INTELLIGENCE SUMMARY.

(Erase heading not required.)

Instructions regarding War Diaries and Intelligence Summaries are contained in F. S. Regs., Part II. and the Staff Manual respectively. Title pages will be prepared in manuscript.

Place	Date	Hour	Summary of Events and Information	Remarks and references to Appendices
DOULLENS	1.9.16		Mobile Veterinary Station proceeds to LE CAUROY.	
LE CAUROY	2.9.16		Proceeded to LE CAUROY on strength of D.N.Q. Arranged to take over position of 21st Div. M.V.1. at AGNEZ-LEZ-DUISANS. Interviewed A.D.V.S. 21st Div. at DUISANS.	
"	3.9.16		Inspected 107th & 105th Field Ambulances. 107th horses condition good; shoeing fair 105th " " " ; " insufficient forage; shoeing insufficient.	
"	4.9.16		Sent Range A.V.C. admittal sick to 106th F. Ambulance.	
"	5.9.16		Proceeded to DUISANS with D.N.Q.	
"	6.9.16		Inspected sick horses at Mobile Veterinary Station for evacuation to Rear. Arranged with C.R.E. to erect shelter for M.V.1.	

T2134. Wt. W708-776. 500000. 4/15. Sir J. C. & S.

Army Form C. 2118.

WAR DIARY
or
INTELLIGENCE SUMMARY.
(Erase heading not required.)

Instructions regarding War Diaries and Intelligence Summaries are contained in F. S. Regs., Part II. and the Staff Manual respectively. Title pages will be prepared in manuscript.

Place	Date	Hour	Summary of Events and Information	Remarks and references to Appendices
BUISANS.	7.9.16		Met D.D.V.S. 3rd Army & inspected 126th F.A. Coy. 37th Division (att. 35th Div.) Horses of A Battery convalescent from influenza needing a period recovery.	
"	8.9.16		Inspected 145th M.G.C. Condition of animals fair; suffering from overwork.	
"	9.9.16		Inspected C Battery 157th F.A. Bde. V.O. reports some cases of lichen front; disease appears to be of a mild form, and cases making a good recovery.	
"	10.9.16		Inspected No.14 Section D.A.C. Condition of animals & shoeing good.	
"	11.9.16		Arranged for erection of water troughs with Lieut. Major DOUGLAS. Inspected sick horses at H.V.E. for evacuation to L.V.C. " another R.A. horses & evacuated 9 debility cases to H.V.S.	

Army Form C. 2118.

WAR DIARY
or
INTELLIGENCE SUMMARY.
(Erase heading not required.)

Instructions regarding War Diaries and Intelligence Summaries are contained in F. S. Regs., Part II. and the Staff Manual respectively. Title pages will be prepared in manuscript.

Place	Date	Hour	Summary of Events and Information	Remarks and references to Appendices
DUISANS.	12.9.16		Inspected 150th F.A. Bde.	
			A Battery. Horses condition fair; about 15% horses on light condition; shoeing fair.	
			B " " condition fair; shoeing fair.	
			C " " condition good; shoeing good.	
			D " " " good; shoeing good.	
			" " fair; shoeing good.	
			Inspected 107th F.A.Bde. Horses have recovered to M.I.1.	
"	13.9.16		Inspected 203rd F.C. R.E.	
			Condition of animals & shoeing good.	
"	14.9.16		Inspected 204th F.C. R.E.	
			Condition of horses generally good; shoeing fair.	
"	15.9.16		Inspected Horses of VI Corps Cyclists.	
			Condition of animals satisfactory.	
			Inspected 205th F.C. R.E. Condition & shoeing generally good.	

T2134. Wt. W708—776. 500000. 4/15. Sir J. C. & S.

Army Form C. 2118.

WAR DIARY
or
INTELLIGENCE SUMMARY.
(Erase heading not required.)

Instructions regarding War Diaries and Intelligence Summaries are contained in F. S. Regs., Part II. and the Staff Manual respectively. Title pages will be prepared in manuscript.

Place	Date	Hour	Summary of Events and Information	Remarks and references to Appendices
DUISANS	16.9.16		Inspected C Battery 157" F.A. Bde. Took 5 horses with Pelvic fever, symptoms of a mild nature & cases coming on pretty numerous. Total of horses from regiment severe pneumonia. A Battery 157 F.A. Bde.: Pelvic fever above 15% in light condition. B " " " " " : " " " " Health generally good & better government. D " " " " " : " " " "	
"	17.9.16		Three mules A/Lng 6 Williams, Howe & Gilmore sent to No. 2 Veterinary Hospital, HAVRE. Lieut E. Selsburg reported for duty & is attached to 159" F.A. Bde.	
"	17.9.16		Inspected sick horses at Mobile Veterinary Section for evacuation to L. of C.	
"	18.9.16		Inspected Detail 35" Div. Artillery. Evacuated 2 horses to Mobile Section	

(5)

Army Form C. 2118.

WAR DIARY
or
INTELLIGENCE SUMMARY.
(Erase heading not required.)

Instructions regarding War Diaries and Intelligence Summaries are contained in F. S. Regs., Part II. and the Staff Manual respectively. Title pages will be prepared in manuscript.

Place	Date	Hour	Summary of Events and Information	Remarks and references to Appendices
DUISANS	19.9.16		Inspected 159th F.A. Amb. Condition generally good; horses taken over from 163rd Amb. in slight condition. 150th F.A.B. Amb. B.C. & D. Batteries generally good; about 15% in slight condition. A battery condition good; of previous load.	
"	20.9.16		Accompanied D.D.V.S. 3rd Army on his inspection of 157th, 158th & 159th F.A. Ambs.	
"	21.9.16		Inspected sick horses at Mobile Vet. Section for evacuation to L.S.C.	
"	22.9.16		Accompanied D.D.V.S. on his inspection of :— 104th, 105th & 106th Infy. Ambs., M.G. Coy r 203rd, 204th, 205th R.E. Cos. Pioneer 13th	
		3 P.M.	D.D.V.S. inspected D.A.C. horses & mules.	

T/134. Wt. W708—776. 500000. 4/15. Sir J. C. & S.

(6)

Army Form C. 2118.

WAR DIARY
or
INTELLIGENCE SUMMARY.

(Erase heading not required.)

Instructions regarding War Diaries and Intelligence Summaries are contained in F. S. Regs., Part II. and the Staff Manual respectively. Title pages will be prepared in manuscript.

Place	Date	Hour	Summary of Events and Information	Remarks and references to Appendices
DUISANS.	23.9.16		Hospital cuts down at M.D.S. for evacuation to I.Q.C.	
"	24.9.16		Hospital Trains Monter & Roads stone lorries. Condition: fine & frosty morning, wet eveng. 106th F. Ambulance. Condition of wounded good.	
"	25.9.16		Evacuated horses to 741, 26, Don. Trains. Adjutant in charge evacuation of wounded; evacuated sit-sit to M.I.R.1 & walked wounded sit-foot to M.I.R.1. Evacuated No 4, 6, A.T.C. Condition of horses good. 256 Imalling, C. R.E.; one horse evacuation of wounded evacuated to M.I.R.1.	
"	26.9.16		Evacuated sick horses to 159° F.A. Ble. Cavalier evacuated. No 1, 2 x 3, Co. A.T.C. Condition generally good.	

Army Form C. 2118.

WAR DIARY
or
INTELLIGENCE SUMMARY.
(Erase heading not required.)

Instructions regarding War Diaries and Intelligence Summaries are contained in F. S. Regs., Part II. and the Staff Manual respectively. Title pages will be prepared in manuscript.

Place	Date	Hour	Summary of Events and Information	Remarks and references to Appendices
DUISANS	27.9.16		Inspected horses of NEW ZEALAND TUNNELLING Co at ARRAS. Condition satisfactory.	
"	28.9.16		Inspected horses of 109th Fd. Ambulance. Condition generally good.	
			" " 105 " "	
	2.30		" horses of 5th Entrenching Bt. at LUCEZ Condition satisfactory.	
"	29.9.16		Inspected horses at Mobile Veterinary Section for evacuation. Sent home of 159 to A. Rds.	
"	30.9.16		Presented to No 5 Veterinary Hospital & saw process of clipping horses &c. also system of disinfection &c &ct.	

W.N. Taylor. Major A.V.C.
A.D.V.S. 35th Div.

Army Form C. 2118.

WAR DIARY of A.D.V.S. 35th Div.
INTELLIGENCE SUMMARY
(Erase heading not required.)

Instructions regarding War Diaries and Intelligence Summaries are contained in F.S. Regs., Part II. and the Staff Manual respectively. Title pages will be prepared in manuscript.

Vol 9

A.D.V.S. No. 517 Date 5/11/16 35th DIVISION

Place	Date	Hour	Summary of Events and Information	Remarks and references to Appendices
SAMS	1.10.16		Evacuated sick horses at Mobile Veterinary Section for evacuation to L.S.C.	
"	2.10.16		Inspected horses of 35th Signal Co. Condition of horses & harness generally good; animals made shelters.	
"	3.10.16		Two horses belonging to M. LOUIS MARVILLE, No 5 GOUVES reported by V.G. of town, as suffering from skin affection; destruction of horses ordered by M. DAMBRINE, VETERINAIRE of GOMEZ. Same burned of carcases being carried out satisfactorily. Farm placed out of bounds.	
"	4.10.16		Inspected horses & mules of 16th Chshire Condition generally good; during fair. animals of the 9th Gloucester Condition of mules good; L.D. horses fair; animals of 15th Offm Notts + Derby. Condition of mules good; L.D. horses condition light.	

T.134. Wt. W708—776. 500000. 4/15. Sir J. C. & S.

WAR DIARY or INTELLIGENCE SUMMARY

Place	Date	Hour	Summary of Events and Information	Remarks and references to Appendices
DUISANS	4.10.16		Inspected horses & mules of 105th M.P.C. Condition & grooming fair. All serviced made billets. D.D.V.S. inspected horses at No.5 GOUVES in morning & visited the cases of glanders reported on 3.10.16. Received instructions that all civilian horses at GOUVES should be tested with mallein when 35 Div horses. Arranged with M.H.R.G of GOUVES to have all civilian horses paraded for testing at 5 PM, 5.10.16 at the church.	
"	5.10.16		Assisted V.O. of horses with mallein testing of 35th Div horses, together with 29 civilian horses & 2 donkeys belonging to the inhabitants.	
"	6.10.16	4 PM.	Inspected all horses, mules mallein test. No signs of any reactions.	
"	7.10.16		Met II Corps Engineer & selected a site for "Horse clipping hutt" at WANQUENTIN. V.O reports on return from Mallein test of the 5.10.16.	

Army Form C. 2118.

WAR DIARY
or
INTELLIGENCE SUMMARY.
(Erase heading not required.)

Instructions regarding War Diaries and Intelligence Summaries are contained in F. S. Regs., Part II. and the Staff Manual respectively. Title pages will be prepared in manuscript.

Place	Date	Hour	Summary of Events and Information	Remarks and references to Appendices
DOULLENS.	8.10.16		Leave to ENGLAND granted from 9th to 18th Oct. O.C. 45th Mobile Veterinary Section to do duty during that period.	
"	9.10.16		Return of Wellies that forwarded to D.D.V.S. 3rd Army.	
"	10.10.16		Reports sick horses at M.H.1. for examination to Z.V.G.C.	
"	11.10.16		Sun Surgeon to A.V.C. reported deficient to D.D.V.S.	
"	12.10.16		Reports horses & mules of 19th Northumberland Fusiliers unfit for Army front.	
"	13.10.16		Reports horses of 203rd F.C. R.E. at LUVEZ unfit for Army front; shoeing fair; animals made skeltes.	
"	14.10.16		Reports 208th F.C. R.E. unfit for Army front; shoeing good.	

T-134. Wt. W708-776. 500000. 4/15. Sir J. C. & S.

(H)

Army Form C. 2118.

WAR DIARY
or
INTELLIGENCE SUMMARY.
(Erase heading not required.)

Instructions regarding War Diaries and Intelligence Summaries are contained in F. S. Regs., Part II. and the Staff Manual respectively. Title pages will be prepared in manuscript.

Place	Date	Hour	Summary of Events and Information	Remarks and references to Appendices
DUISANS	15.10.16		Capt Gordon A.V.C. att. 106 Fly Abe proc to leave to ENGLAND.	
"	16.10.16		Reports sick horses at Mobile Veterinary Section for evacuation to L. of C.	
"	17.10.16		Reports 205' F. C. R.E. Conduct & moral good; L.D. Good; showing front	
"	18.10.16		12 horses arrived from leave to D.P.V.T.	
"	19.10.16		Reports the following commands attached:— VI Corps Cyclists & 11" Div. Cyclists. 2" Glamorgan Army Troops L. R.E. & 8" Field Survey Co. Conditn of commands generally water & feeding; All erected shelters at R.E. dump DUISANS.	
"	20.10.16		Reports 15" Chapman. 3 H.D. Horses in bright condition & require extra attention. Commenced clipping Mules legs & proceeds them out to transport officers on such function.	

T2134. Wt. W708—776. 500000. 4/15. Sir J. C. & S.

Army Form C. 2118.

WAR DIARY
or
INTELLIGENCE SUMMARY.
(Erase heading not required.)

Instructions regarding War Diaries and Intelligence Summaries are contained in F. S. Regs., Part II. and the Staff Manual respectively. Title pages will be prepared in manuscript.

Place	Date	Hour	Summary of Events and Information	Remarks and references to Appendices
DUISANS	20.10.16		Horses under first lines. Reports 84. 9.6. 105° Bde. Condition of animals satisfactory. Reports Q.Q. cable section, 5° Army Corps. Condition of animals satisfactory. Relate to Veterinary Dressing for this unit.	
"	21.10.16		Reports 157° F.A. Bde. A. Bty horses, condition fair; A sub-section condition poor; grooming poor. B " " " condition fair; grooming poor. D " " " " ; grooming bad. C " " " " ; four cases of influenza in said horses. One case of Ram glac mange found in this Battery (13 sub-section) + evacuated to M.V.S.	
"	22.10.16		Reports Bdt. 26. 104° Infy. Bde.; Condition of horses under first lines. N.D. horses of 103° Bde in poor condition.	

Army Form C. 2118.

WAR DIARY
or
INTELLIGENCE SUMMARY.
(Erase heading not required.)

Instructions regarding War Diaries and Intelligence Summaries are contained in F. S. Regs., Part II. and the Staff Manual respectively. Title pages will be prepared in manuscript.

Place	Date	Hour	Summary of Events and Information	Remarks and references to Appendices
DUISANS	22.10.16		Infantry 23rd Manchester; Arrived in good condition; showing fair	
		20	„ L. Fusiliers „ „ „ „ „	
		10	„ „ „ „ fair condition.	
		17	„ „ „ „ „	
		„	Much improvement; N.D. leaves in light condition.	
		10 H M.G.C.; Arrived generally in good condition; showing fair	
"	23.10.16		Infantry 35th D.A.C.	
			No 1. Section; Battalion brought into Infantry; about 10 %; in light condition.	
			„ 2 „ „ Condition ; Bad; about 15 %; in light condition.	
			„ 3 „ „ „ generally good.	
			„ 4 „ „ Much very (scarce); showing B D.A.C.; fair; generally in fair fairing	
			No 2 & 3 Section Shelter not yet completed.	
"	24.10.16		Infantry Horses of 159th F.A. Bde.	
			A. Battery ; condition generally good.	
			B. „ „ „ „ „	

Army Form C. 2118.

WAR DIARY
or
INTELLIGENCE SUMMARY.
(Erase heading not required.)

Instructions regarding War Diaries and Intelligence Summaries are contained in F. S. Regs., Part II. and the Staff Manual respectively. Title pages will be prepared in manuscript.

Place	Date	Hour	Summary of Events and Information	Remarks and references to Appendices
DIV:A:H.S.	24/10/16		Emplacements C. Pitting; condition fair; about 6'½ hours in Right condition	
			" D " ; condition good.	
			Shining generally satisfactory.	
			Water troughs for Other Brigade not yet complete; intend it to 2nd Div. R.A.	
"	25.10.16		Emplacements 150° F.A. 12 Bde.	
			A. Battery, condition fair; ammunition fair arrangements this recommend them shown to N.C.O.	
			B " " " fair; ditto had refused to R.A.	
			C " " " good	
			D " " " good	
			Shining generally satisfactory;	
			Saw n/c 1 Water troughs have been but approved; recommend R.A. to remove them.	
"	26.10.16		Emplacements M.G.C. A.T.C.	
			Condition fair not uniform; about 16 these horses that require more attention.	
			" " " M.G.C A.T.C. Condition good.	

WAR DIARY
or
INTELLIGENCE SUMMARY.

Army Form C. 2118.

Place	Date	Hour	Summary of Events and Information	Remarks and references to Appendices
OUISANS	27/10/16		Ronfrete No. 3. C. A.T.C. Condition of horses fair	
			No. 4 C. A.T.C	
			Condition of horses poor	
		3 p.m	Shoeing of lame horses by order. Marching of V.6. at N.K.T	
"	28/10/16		Ronfrete Sept 25. 106th Infy Bde. Exhibition of anound equipment	
			" 17th Royal Scots ; anounts fine ; short 5 throws & 3 much oxygen consumption	
			" 17th West. Yorks ; anounts fine ; exhibition very good	
			" 19. D.L.I. "	
			" 18. N.F "	
			" 106th M.G.Co. " several anounts in light condition	
			" " " " men much faster too long, which seem pointless	
			ent- to hospital Bapeau	
"	29.10.16		Ronfrete 106th F.Ambulance ; Condition of anounts extra fair/every	

Army Form C. 2118.

WAR DIARY
or
INTELLIGENCE SUMMARY.
(Erase heading not required.)

Place	Date	Hour	Summary of Events and Information	Remarks and references to Appendices.
DUISANS	30.10.16		Prospects. 105th H. Battalion	
			Condition of ammunition, fuzing; driving fine.	
			107th H. Battalion.	
			Condition of shells, ammunition fuzing; driving fine.	
		31.10.16	Prospects. animals of 16th Battalion; condition of ammunition, good; driving fine.	
			" 14th Gloucester Bde.; condition of ammunition fuzing; 2nd Horses too light condition; driving fine.	
			" 15th Bde. HQ to Bde. Party; condition of saddle good; Relics very good.	
			2nd Horses out good & supervises. Batter feeding; driving fine.	
			" 105th M.G.C. condition good; driving fine; some feet overgrown.	

W.H. Leigh Major A.V.C.
A.D.V.S. 35th Div.

Army Form C. 2118.

WAR DIARY of ADVC. 35th Div.
or
INTELLIGENCE SUMMARY.
(Erase heading not required.)

Vol 10

Place	Date	Hour	Summary of Events and Information	Remarks and references to Appendices
BUISANS	1.11.16		Inspected sick lines of 35th Divisional Ammunition Column. Casualties about the average. Inspected remounts of DAC; Inspected G. & M.M.P. Condition good.	
"	2.11.16		Inspected 205th Fld Co. R.E. Condition generally good: L.D front. 204th Fld Co. R.E. Condition of horses good: Shoeing satisfactory. Examined 59 Remounts opening 159th & 169th Bdes Condition generally good; drawn horses aged 15 to 16 years.	
"	3.11.16		Inspected horses at No. 2 Sec. 47th Bgde. R.G.A. Condition satisfactory.	
		3.P.M.	Conference (small) of V.Os at Mobile Veterinary Section.	

Army Form C. 2118.

WAR DIARY
or
INTELLIGENCE SUMMARY.
(Erase heading not required.)

Instructions regarding War Diaries and Intelligence Summaries are contained in F. S. Regs., Part II. and the Staff Manual respectively. Title pages will be prepared in manuscript.

Place	Date	Hour	Summary of Events and Information	Remarks and references to Appendices
OUISNES.	4.11.16		Inspected sick horses at Mobile Section for evacuation to hospital.	
"	5.11.16		Inspected D Troop 3rd Pontoon Park. Condition of horses generally good. New standings in open shelter are being erected.	
			19th Northumberland Fusiliers. Condition of animals good; shoeing fair.	
"	6.11.16		Inspected French Mortar & Bomb store horses. Five horses in light condition, others satisfactory.	
"	7.11.16		Inspected a series of stations in places belonging to 157th F.A. Bde. Care of horses satisfactory.	

Army Form C. 2118.

WAR DIARY
or
INTELLIGENCE SUMMARY.
(Erase heading not required.)

Instructions regarding War Diaries and Intelligence Summaries are contained in F. S. Regs., Part II. and the Staff Manual respectively. Title pages will be prepared in manuscript.

Place	Date	Hour	Summary of Events and Information	Remarks and references to Appendices
DUISANS.	8.11.16		Reported horses & mules of 35" Reserve Co. arrived in good condition; showing extra frostion. O.C. 45" Mobile Veterinary Section granted leave to England.	
"	9.11.16		Reported horse No 1. Indian D.V.C. reported as suffering from skin abrasions, animal isolated for examination & further observation.	
"	10.11.16	3 P.M.	Weekly conference of V.Os at Mobile Veterinary Section.	
"	11.11.16		Reported 6 cast horses for evacuation to hospital.	
"	12.11.16		A case of lymphitis amongst draught in 204" F.C. R.E. & evacuated to M.V.S. Reported all horses of 'company' & found no further cases of a suspicious nature.	
"	13.11.16		Reported 203" F.C. R.E. Horses & Mules in good condition; showing wits for Army.	

T.1134. Wt. W708—776. 500000. 4/15. Sir J. C. & S.

WAR DIARY
or
INTELLIGENCE SUMMARY.
(Erase heading not required.)

Army Form C. 2118.

Place	Date	Hour	Summary of Events and Information	Remarks and references to Appendices
BOULOGNE	14.10.16		Evacuated 17 sick monals from M.V.I. to Hospital. Inspected a house of No.1. Section D.A.C. infected with skin disease; men sent out for to be examined. Capt. M. Walker A.V.C. admitted sick to Field Ambulance, report sent to D.D.V.S. 2ⁿᵈ Army.	
"	15.11.16		Inspected sick animals among the 105ᵗʰ & 106ᵗʰ Infantry Bdes. Evacuated 1. N.D. from 15ᵗʰ Chesshires. " " " " D.A.C. " " " K.D. " Casualties about the average.	
"	16.11.16		Inspected No.1. Co. A.S.C. Condition of animals fair; about 10 horses in too light a condition; showing from I put out to G.C. Farm.	

Army Form C. 2118.

WAR DIARY
or
INTELLIGENCE SUMMARY
(Erase heading not required.)

Instructions regarding War Diaries and Intelligence Summaries are contained in F.S. Regs., Part II. and the Staff Manual respectively. Title Pages will be prepared in manuscript.

Place	Date	Hour	Summary of Events and Information	Remarks and references to Appendices
DUISANS	17/1/16		Inspected Gun Park Horses of 150" F.A. Bde. Ammunition about normal. Horses of A Battery too emaciated; reported this to C.R.A. Medical conference of V.G. at Mobile Veterinary Section.	
"	18/1/16		Inspected sick animals at Mobile Veterinary Section for evacuation to hospital.	
"	19/1/16		Inspected N.B. Horses belonging to R.T.E. A used of functional leg as a result to find; ordered its destruction.	
"	20/1/16		Inspected D. Hunt 3" Pattern Pack at support of Transport Officer. Condition of horses rather poor. Now major deletion. There horses under the condition unimproved. Recommended C.R.E. to [give] these horses until their condition improved. Inspected 500" Howitzer Bty. att. 159" F.A. Bde. 12 Bty. left ENGLAND on 1" Nov. Condition of animals proved poor. Picketed in the open. Recommended them to use May meb. Met D.D.R. 3" Army for canting B - 5 Remount teams.	

2449 Wt. W14957/M90 750,000 1/16 J.B.C. & A. Forms/C.2118/12.

Army Form C. 2118.

WAR DIARY
or
INTELLIGENCE SUMMARY

(Erase heading not required.)

Place	Date	Hour	Summary of Events and Information	Remarks and references to Appendices
DOISANS	21/1/16		Refuted Cope sent to R.E. Dump; 1st Lancs. 32nd Horse Rd. Limbers to ammunition front 14th Army F.C. R.E. Limber to ammunition point 2nd Glamorgan Co. R.E. Limber to ammunition front	
"	22/1/16		Refuted Billets 21st Mobile Veterinary Section and the F.C. 45th M.V.S.	
"	23/1/16		Refuted 95th Divisional Ammunition Column. M.O.I. declared horses in good condition; under shelter " 2 " " " " about 12 mounted in light condition; no shelter " 3 " " " " " 15 " " " " " (part under shelter)	
"	24/1/16		Weekly conference of V.Os at Mobile Veterinary Section Spoon Demonstration. To mullein dose to N.Cos (Potter-Vermule published methods.)	

Army Form C. 2118.

WAR DIARY
or
INTELLIGENCE SUMMARY
(Erase heading not required.)

Place	Date	Hour	Summary of Events and Information	Remarks and references to Appendices
QUISAMS	25/11/16		Received by wire from Infantry HdQrs instructions in course of advancing with the Divisional HdQrs. Main convoy forward the tent.	
"	26/11/16		Ramfutta with horses for evacuation to Ramfutta	
"	27/11/16		Ramfutta Horses & 157° F.A. Rgt. Cavalry & A. 12th horses. " B " " " C " " " D " " Powering Forces. All under shelter. Carts very rough	
"	30/11/16		Ramfutta Horses & 158° F.A. 12th Rgt. Cavalry 12th Cavalry forces; post reinforcement. " B " " " " C " " " D " " Powering forces Carts very rough. All under shelter. Powering forces	

WAR DIARY
or
INTELLIGENCE SUMMARY

(Erase heading not required.)

Army Form C. 2118.

Place	Date	Hour	Summary of Events and Information	Remarks and references to Appendices
DOISANS	29/11/16		Perfecta Round 15. 159° F.A. Bde. A. 135 Crater generally good B. " " very good C. " " fair D. " " generally good; Shrining fair. All ammo skeleton.	
"	30/11/16		Arrived K6 of to Mallein 500" Howitzer Perfecta 106° F. Howitzer One have was erratic to M.V.L. inferior to Rough &tr. average. " 105° F. Howitzer Crater of round good; showing satisfactory.	

3.12.16

W.N. Layton, Major. R.G.
O.C. 35. Bns.

Army Form C. 2118.

WAR DIARY of A.D.V.S. 35° Div.
or
INTELLIGENCE SUMMARY   ADVS 352

(Erase heading not required.)

Vol XI

Instructions regarding War Diaries and Intelligence
Summaries are contained in F. S. Regs., Part II.
and the Staff Manual respectively. Title Pages
will be prepared in manuscript.

Place	Date	Hour	Summary of Events and Information	Remarks and references to Appendices
BUISANS	1.12.16		Weekly conference of V.Os at Mobile Veterinary Section. Inspected sick horse lines the 105th & 106th Infantry Bde. Evacuated 1 Mule from 19th N.Z.P. " 1 " from 106th Bde H.Q.	
"	2.12.16		Inspected sick animals & lines of 104th Infantry Bde. Convalescents arrived.	
"	3.12.16		Inspected sick horses at Mobile Veterinary Section for evacuation to hospital.	
"	4.12.16		Inspected animals of 204th F.C. R.E. Condition: good; showing fair.	
"	5.12.16		Proceeded to ROELLECOURT in charge of D.H.D.	
ROELLECOURT	6.12.16		Inspected No. 3 C. A. & C. Horses in good condition; acute shelter; floor requires matting. Watering from troughs at in froncis.	

WAR DIARY or INTELLIGENCE SUMMARY

Army Form C. 2118.

(Erase heading not required.)

Place	Date	Hour	Summary of Events and Information	Remarks and references to Appendices
ROELLECOURT	6.12.16		Inspected Bn. 25 annual 1/7" Northumberland Fusiliers & W & X Coys. Arrived in very good condition; whole battalion; Watching from troops at front.	
			Inspected 105th Fd. Ambulance. Arrived in horses. Conditions good; Watching from front.	
			" 205 F.C. R.E. Arrived in good condition; stabled in horses.	
			" 203 F.C. R.E. Arrived in good condition; mules & billets; watching from front.	
			" 106 F. Ambulance. Arrived in good condition; stabled in horses; watching from front.	
"	7.12.16		Inspected 106 Fd. Bn. 25. Arrived on attack; condition satisfactory.	
			" 106 M.G. Co. 50 to animals, mules & billets; condition fair; glorie of rebellion anywhere in being.	
			" 17 N.T.F.: Condition of animal fair; stabled in horses; watching from front.	

Army Form C. 2118.

WAR DIARY
or
INTELLIGENCE SUMMARY

(Erase heading not required.)

Instructions regarding War Diaries and Intelligence Summaries are contained in F. S. Regs., Part II. and the Staff Manual respectively. Title Pages will be prepared in manuscript.

Place	Date	Hour	Summary of Events and Information	Remarks and references to Appendices
BELLECOURT	8.12.16		Inspected 15" August by. Horses under shelter; chloroform found. Condition of animals good. No. 1 M.A.S.C. 50% animals on steps of new condition satisfactory; unfit forward from nose.	
"	9.12.16		Inspected and drew from reservation to Rondevilte at Mobile Veterinary Section	
"	10.12.16		Inspected a horse at 106th F. Ambulance affected with otion chronica. Animals suffering in aware; animals inoculated & undergoing treatment. 105th M.T.Co.: Animals fair; dirt of mein large. Arrival in heaven; watering from pond. Condition of animals fair. 15th Cheshires: Condition fair; animals distributed about in different towns; watering from well. 14th Gloucesters: Condition fair; animals in horses; watering from well; bivouacked / horses to Mobile Veterinary Section. 15" Notts v Derby: Arrival in still; watering at pond (bad water); recommended use of well. Condition satisfactory.	

Army Form C. 2118.

WAR DIARY
or
INTELLIGENCE SUMMARY

(Erase heading not required.)

Instructions regarding War Diaries and Intelligence Summaries are contained in F. S. Regs., Part II. and the Staff Manual respectively. Title Pages will be prepared in manuscript.

Place	Date	Hour	Summary of Events and Information	Remarks and references to Appendices
MAILLECOURT	11.12.16		Completed transport arrival of Regd Arts. Exhibition fair: about 6 more lamps; nothing from front. Arrived in Heth.	
"	12.12.16		Weather unsettled. Rode: Rummy during the day. Interviewed D.D.V.S. 3rd Army.	
"	13.12.16		Reported M. & B. A.T.C. Exhibition amplification; Inspection to check motor refuse. Capt. C. F. Thompson A.V.C. from No. 3. Base Remount Depot, reported for duty on strans. Capt. Wilson evacuated sick.	
"	14.12.16		D.D.V.S. 3rd Army inspected 45th Mobile Veterinary Section. Lecture on Horse Management to 107th Battalion asked if inclination.	
"		2 PM		
"	15.12.16		Interviewed O.C. 45th M.V.S. to send Pte BACON. A.V.C. 15 W.O. 2. Veterinary Hosp for its Antwerp D.D.V.S. 3rd Army.	

Army Form C. 2118.

WAR DIARY
or
INTELLIGENCE SUMMARY

(Erase heading not required.)

Instructions regarding War Diaries and Intelligence Summaries are contained in F. S. Regs., Part II. and the Staff Manual respectively. Title Pages will be prepared in manuscript.

Place	Date	Hour	Summary of Events and Information	Remarks and references to Appendices
ROELLECOURT	16.12.16		Inspected 2 cases of skin disease at D. 159" F.A. Bde. Cases diagnosed at Mange & and sent to 21st Mobile Veterinary Section.	
			Inspt. Mc Intosh sent to No. 2 Veterinary Hospital for further training. Authority D.D.V.S. 3rd Army.	
"	17.12.16		Inspected horses at 45th Mobile Veterinary Section for evacuation to hospital.	
"	18.12.16		Inspected animals of 105" F. Ambulance. Condition good, showing signs	
"	19.12.16		Returned in Reconnaissance to 15" Dn. M. Gs & Duty.	
"	20.12.16		" at Div. 2 Hr. 14" Pioneers.	
"	21.12.16		V.G. outputs seven cases Inspected Mange belonging to 106" F. Ambulance. All animals isolated. 2 Mules & 1 Plate evacuated on suspicion.	

2449 Wt. W14957/M90 750,000 1/16 J.B.C. & A. Forms/C.2118/12.

WAR DIARY
or
INTELLIGENCE SUMMARY
(Erase heading not required.)

Army Form C. 2118.

Place	Date	Hour	Summary of Events and Information	Remarks and references to Appendices
MIELLECOURT	22.12.16		Lectures on Horsemanagement at Hd.Qrs. 17th Rompt Pork.	
"	23.12.16		Inspected sick horses at 45 M.V.1. for evacuation. Lecture on Horsemanagement at 14.12.6. 10" Driffield 2. Infantry.	
"	24.12.16		Issued trypsin particulars of places put "out of Bounds" for Brks & Horses at Office of D.D.V.S. 1st Army.	
"	25.12.16		Routine.	
"	26.12.16		4/1/Cdn. Stand. M.V.C. attached to No. 3 Rn. Fn. D.A.C.	
"	27.12.16		Investigated the collection of horse bones on 26 Nov 16 by No. 3 Veterinary Mobile Section from M. HOQUET at OEUF; arranging to interview from D.D.V.S. M. HOQUET reports that these were never removed of "Motor Ambulance".	

Army Form C. 2118.

WAR DIARY
or
INTELLIGENCE SUMMARY

(Erase heading not required.)

Instructions regarding War Diaries and Intelligence Summaries are contained in F. S. Regs., Part II. and the Staff Manual respectively. Title Pages will be prepared in manuscript.

Place	Date	Hour	Summary of Events and Information	Remarks and references to Appendices
ROELLECOURT	28.12.16		Reported 106" F. Ambulance arrived. No further news of action scheme.	
"	29.12.16		Reported Horse Lines to 159" F.A. Bde. Overall facilities in the open on hard bye roads. Water troughs improvised in front.	
"	30.12.16		Reported 106" M.G.C. Arrived in good condition.	
"	31.12.16		Reported D. Battery 159" F.A. Bde. Arrived in good condition. No further news of action scheme detected.	

W.N. Vaughan
Major A.V.C.

1.1.17

CONFIDENTIAL

WAR DIARY of ADVT. 35th Div.
or
INTELLIGENCE SUMMARY

Army Form C. 2118

Vol 12

Place	Date	Hour	Summary of Events and Information	Remarks and references to Appendices
ROELLECOURT	1.1.17		Reports Return of No. 2 Co. A.T.C. Condition generally good: mules & battus: continuing free trough at front. Reported W.L.W. & M 2 tr. 19th Northumbd Fusiliers. Animals in good condition; mules & battus. 105" F. Ambulance horses. " " Pltrs & horses: Condition very good.	
"	2.1.17		Reports 19th 19th West Ptn. Condition of animals good: mules & battus. 19th Bn. D.L.I.: Condition of animals good: mules & battus.	
"	3.1.17		Reports No. 1 Co. A.T.C. Condition of horses generally good: Watering from trough at front. Animals in stables & shelter.	
"	4.1.17		Reports Details of 35th D.A.C. after reorganisation. Evacuated 26 horses to Remts for poor condition. Remainy horses & mules in good condition. Mules in boot standings with cover.	

WAR DIARY
or
INTELLIGENCE SUMMARY

(Erase heading not required.)

Army Form C. 2118

Place	Date	Hour	Summary of Events and Information	Remarks and references to Appendices
ROELLECOURT	5.1.17		Reported Personnel A, B & C. Batteries 150' F.A. Bde at MONTENESCOURT. Awaits for parade. All animals made available; Officers anxiously assembling.	
"	6.1.17		Reported @ Resting Horses 150' F.A. Bde at HUNVAL. Conditions good; standing on hard ground. Watering from trough at station.	
"	7.1.17		Reported sick animals at M.V.S. for evacuation to Prosfeld.	
"	8.1.17		Reported W. H. & L. W. D. C. Condition of animals good; stabled in sheds & barns. Watering from trough at ponds.	
"	9.1.17		Reported Personnel to W.C. 19th Westmoreland Fusiliers. Condition satisfactory. Horses attached to Depot Pln. Condition satisfactory; Personnel requires more attention.	

Army Form C. 2118

WAR DIARY
or
INTELLIGENCE SUMMARY
(Erase heading not required.)

Place	Date	Hour	Summary of Events and Information	Remarks and references to Appendices
ROELLECOURT	10.4.19		Reported arrival to 106 Fd. Ambulance. M. for the man to Minorge: Sun remained under observation. Evacuation proceeding properly. Reported 203 F.E.R.E. Whole six months on the floor; lines very muddy; Matches need mending for accomodation. Condition satisfactory.	
"	11.4.19		Reported Nos. 1 & 2. Stations D.W.C. at BOURET. Chemical firebats to be sent to line on lys avant; position rather exposed; had retaining. Condition of No. 1. Station unmarked D.Q.R. No. 2. " Ehime. Water: hour: expose myself more attention to later finishing; Recommended shelter for them. Recommended to hurries to hospital for disability.	
"	12.1.19		Examined R.M. on N.O. Rumer died belonging to No. 2. C.C.S.C. Cause of death, strangulation of intestine.	
"	13.1.19		Reported sick Rumer at M.Y.A. for examination to hospital.	

WAR DIARY
or
INTELLIGENCE SUMMARY

Army Form C. 2118

Place	Date	Hour	Summary of Events and Information	Remarks and references to Appendices
ROELLECOURT 14.1.17	15.1.17		Reported arrival of N. 2. C. M. T. C. at HABARCQ. Condition on leaving: Under shelter. Four cases of Ponctus arrange movements to Ponctus.	
"			Reported 17th Punisher Pounder at AGNEZ. Condition good: stabled in sheds. 16th Elenturies " Condition good: En shelter. Lorry lorries of A & B Batteries 159th Bde at MONTENESCOURT. Condition under fontery.	
"	16.1.17		Reported Return of 1st Cavalry Pioneer Pln. All animals under cover & condition under footery. Arrangements for guards.	
"	17.1.17		Reported Pleuro for exercise at M.V.T. Heavy fall of snow during the day. 1 Remount placed for horse transport.	

WAR DIARY
or
INTELLIGENCE SUMMARY

Army Form C. 2118

(Erase heading not required.)

Instructions regarding War Diaries and Intelligence Summaries are contained in F. S. Regs., Part II. and the Staff Manual respectively. Title Pages will be prepared in manuscript.

Place	Date	Hour	Summary of Events and Information	Remarks and references to Appendices
ROELLECOURT	18.1.17		Band front : Bomb Cart for transport. Perfected A. Battery Wagon 159 Pdr. Horses standing in open : Limbers under fcutting. Perfected A. Battery Horses 159 Pdr. Standing in the open : Limbers under fcutting. Perfected all Horses at ROELLECOURT marked "Planters & Wragup" after examination of Front Army. Horses correctly fitted with harness that were than overfired of horses.	
"	19.1.17		Perfected buildings at MAIZIERES Placed. Majority of Horses Hanes no accommodation for animals. Horses continues bad.	
"	20.1.17		Remitted at Count to Engineers in regard to all required belongs to 3rd Army troops by General Veterinary Army.	

Army Form C. 2118

WAR DIARY
or
INTELLIGENCE SUMMARY
(Erase heading not required.)

Instructions regarding War Diaries and Intelligence Summaries are contained in F. S. Regs., Part II. and the Staff Manual respectively. Title Pages will be prepared in manuscript.

Place	Date	Hour	Summary of Events and Information	Remarks and references to Appendices
ROEUX COURT	21.1.17		Prepared and drew horses for evacuation to hospital. Horses continue bad for transport.	
"	22.1.17		Prepared horses of M. 2. 6. A.T.C. Three horses of light weights & unmounted spinal feeding. Others notice fracture. Horses attached to Depot Vet. Condition poor but response more responsive.	
"	23.1.17		Lieut. T. Salisbury A.V.C. evacuated to 106th Field Ambulance on 19th January & unfit to be evacuated to Rouen to duty. Report sent to D.D.V.S.	
"	24.1.17		Reported 203rd F. C. R.E. Animals under shelter; condition generally satisfactory. 18th N. F. P. Animals stabled in barns at several farms; condition satisfactory; standards requires better cleaning. 104th M.G.C. Condition of animals satisfactory; stabled in barns. Horses requires overhauling.	

Army Form C. 2118

WAR DIARY
or
INTELLIGENCE SUMMARY

(Erase heading not required.)

Instructions regarding War Diaries and Intelligence Summaries are contained in F.S. Regs., Part II. and the Staff Manual respectively. Title Pages will be prepared in manuscript.

Place	Date	Hour	Summary of Events and Information	Remarks and references to Appendices
ROELLECOURT	25·1·17		Reported 157 F.A. Bde. Remove at MONTENESCOURT. Horses made shelter with benefit of one section B Battery. Condition rather fair/poor. " B. Battery 159 F.A. Bde. Condition fairly good; harness Bd. 1 team of shelter to MVI. Horses made shelter.	
"	26·1·17		Conference of A.Q.D. V.S. at 3rd Army.	
"	29·1·17		D.D.V.S. inspected 45th M.V.S.	
"	30·1·17		Reported to A, C, D, Batteries 159 F.A. Bde. Animals made cover & condition rather fair/poor. " 15th Division. Animals in very good condition. " N.T.S. at GOUVES. Several animals in poor condition; Majority of animals made shelter. " Royal Fusiliers at GOUVES; Animal covered in poor condition.	

1875 Wt. W593/826 1,000,000 4/15 J.B.C. & A. A.D.S.S./Forms/C. 2118.

WAR DIARY
or
INTELLIGENCE SUMMARY

(Erase heading not required.)

Army Form C. 2118

Place	Date	Hour	Summary of Events and Information	Remarks and references to Appendices
RIBEMONT	29/1/17		Inspected 205' of R.E. at BRAY. Emulsion of mineral jelly installed in shelters. " 35" D.W.C. at WANQUETIN. No. 1. Anti-toxin serum deposit in good condition. " 2 " " " " " 3 " Much in good condition. All under shelter.	
"	30/1/17		Inspected 106" M.F.C. Exhibits of mineral water pouring.	
"	31/1/17		Collected a sick horse from HAIRE & COUTEVILLE. Left by 39' Div 179 Bde on 25'Mar'16 Horse transport took the horse at " " " according to instructions received from Q.DVI. 3'Army	

W.N. Singleton Major AVC
ADVO / 35 Div

Army Form C. 2118

WAR DIARY A.D.V.S. 35th Div.
INTELLIGENCE SUMMARY

Vol / 3

(Erase heading not required.)

Instructions regarding War Diaries and Intelligence Summaries are contained in F.S. Regs., Part II. and the Staff Manual respectively. Title Pages will be prepared in manuscript.

Place	Date	Hour	Summary of Events and Information	Remarks and references to Appendices
NOELLECOURT	1.2.17		Reported Rear & made to 109th F. Ambulance. Horse drawn Lorry died of Contagious Pneumonia. Numerous other to be examined. Diagnosis turned out.	
"	2.2.17		Reported 1st Cavalry Division H.Q. Three cases earmarked for Mange: One case earmarked for Debility. Condition of animals general on the factory. Three cases of Abnormalities Contagious reported in Right Section C/159 Bde. R.F.A. Saw them sent on to continuing of horses. Reported same to D.D.V.S.	
	3.2.17		Reported Right Section Rear C/159 Bde R.F.A. on further cases of Mange below found. Arranged for affected horses to be further seen by 12th Div. M.V.S. when history numbered.	
	4.2.17		No further cases at ST. POL. Arranged to ammunate cases to 9 Dv. M.V.S. at AUBIGNY.	

1875 Wt. W593/826 1,000,000 4/15 J.B.C. & A. A.D.S.S./Forms/C. 2118.

WAR DIARY
or
INTELLIGENCE SUMMARY

Army Form C. 2118

(Erase heading not required.)

Instructions regarding War Diaries and Intelligence Summaries are contained in F. S. Regs., Part II. and the Staff Manual respectively. Title Pages will be prepared in manuscript.

Place	Date	Hour	Summary of Events and Information	Remarks and references to Appendices
ROELLECOURT	5.2.17		Remounts sick remained to to 21st M.V.S.	
BOUQUEMAISON	6.2.17		Remounts with D.H.Q. to BOUQUEMAISON. 45' M.V.S. marched to BEAUREUVE.	
VIGNACOURT	7.2.17		Remounts with D.H.Q. to VIGNACOURT. 45' M.V.S. marched to OCCOCHES.	
"	8.2.17		45' M.V.S. marched to HAVERNAS. Weather intensive frost and snow. Divisional Artillery practised in the open.	
"	9.2.17		Photos: 197th F. & R.E.; Annual practice in the open; Cubicle water factory. 206 F & R.E. & 205 F.G.R.E. Annual practice in the open; Cubicle water factory. 15 Mtd Pttn.d Yeomantsn.; Annual in Rooms; Cubicle water factory. 19 Mtd Ranged Park; Annual in Rooms; Cubicle frame.	

1875 Wt. W593/826 1,000,000 4/15 J.B.C. & A. A.D.S.S./Forms/C. 2118.

WAR DIARY
or
INTELLIGENCE SUMMARY

(Erase heading not required.)

Army Form C. 2118

Instructions regarding War Diaries and Intelligence Summaries are contained in F.S. Regs., Part II. and the Staff Manual respectively. Title Pages will be prepared in manuscript.

Place	Date	Hour	Summary of Events and Information	Remarks and references to Appendices
NISMACOURT	9.2.17		Reports 19th Bde D.T.? Wounded in Burma; condition satisfactory. " 106 M.L.W. Wounded in Burma; condition satisfactory. " M.H.L.A.C.: Arrived frostbite in the open; condition poor. " Pte 25 106 Pde Shrapnel wound in scalp; condition good.	
"	10.2.17		Reports Pars to 159 Bty R.F.A: Horse frostbite in the open; condition generally good; both wounds of Horses slight. " Pars to 157 Bde R.F.A: Horses frostbite in the open; condition generally good. " 35 D.A.C: Wounds frostbite in the open; condition fairly good. No 1 " No 2 " " 3 Mules, ponies.	

1875 Wt. W593/826 1,000,000 4/15 J.B.C. & A. A.D.S.S./Forms/C. 2118.

WAR DIARY or INTELLIGENCE SUMMARY

Army Form C. 2118

(Erase heading not required.)

Place	Date	Hour	Summary of Events and Information	Remarks and references to Appendices
HERMICOURT	11.2.17		Infantry with Brown at M.V.A. for innoculation. Front fairly extensive.	
"	12.2.17		Infantry 106th F. Ambulance. Brown & relief. Stomach more appear to be fever from above causes. W.3.C. N.T.E. Arrived early on this stem; battln. fever.	
"	13.2.17		Infantry Mr. Went forth: battn. to ground & made entrenchments; All made shelter. " with " at H.S. M.V.A.	
"	14.2.17		Infantry 107 F. Ambulance arrived. Employer entrenching. 2v/ Lancashires Repeaters here when other divisions made trenches & temp entrenching.	
		2.30 PM	ATTEND Conference at H. Army.	

Army Form C. 2118

WAR DIARY
or
INTELLIGENCE SUMMARY

(Erase heading not required.)

Instructions regarding War Diaries and Intelligence Summaries are contained in F. S. Regs., Part II. and the Staff Manual respectively. Title Pages will be prepared in manuscript.

Place	Date	Hour	Summary of Events and Information	Remarks and references to Appendices
VIGNACOURT	15.2.17		Reported shower made 105" H. Ambrose. Unit letter T conditions satisfactory.	
"	16.2.17		Reported shower at MVA for ammunition for Rupilts.	
"	17.2.17		Lieut. Pannell H.V.C. reported Pannell for duty & is attached to 159" M.A.R.W.	
GUILLAUCOURT	18.2.17		Rewarded to GUILLAUCOURT with D App.	
"	19.2.17		Found billet for M.V.A. near CAIX.	
"	20.2.17		Reported 292 Army Troops Co. R.E. lardition of armed front: Reconnard cliff in town high.	

1875 Wt. W593/826 1,000,000 4/15 J.B.C. & A. A.D.S.S./Forms/C. 2118.

WAR DIARY
or
INTELLIGENCE SUMMARY

(Erase heading not required.)

Army Form C. 2118

Place	Date	Hour	Summary of Events and Information	Remarks and references to Appendices
GUILLAUCOURT	21.8.17		Infantry 35th Div. Transport moving at Replenishing point. Lentiles of ammunition issued.	
CAIX	22.8.17		Moved to CAIX. Infantry supplied to lorries; Shelter for ammunition found. Infantry 9.14 Army Group Co. R.E. Cooked to ammunition lorries.	
"	23.8.17		Infantry 157th & 159th Bde. lorries. Shelter for ammunition to horses. Ammunition dump on road: Water unfit for use. Infantry 105 Fd. Ambulance Sappers installed in a wood. Approach to route through deep mud. Cavalier generally good.	
"	24.8.17		Infantry lorries to 20 gr 20.4 q 20.5 Cos. R.E. Ammunition under shelter: lorries very muddy.	

Army Form C. 2118

WAR DIARY
or
INTELLIGENCE SUMMARY
(Erase heading not required.)

Instructions regarding War Diaries and Intelligence Summaries are contained in F. S. Regs., Part II. and the Staff Manual respectively. Title Pages will be prepared in manuscript.

Place	Date	Hour	Summary of Events and Information	Remarks and references to Appendices
CTIX	25.8.17		Conference Comdts of 35th D.A.C. No. 1 Section in shelters; ammunition coy assembly. " 2 " in farm building; standing gun cover. " 3 " " shelters; standing gun cover. Watering point. Enquired 106th Fd. Ambulance. Demands on shelters. Intends N.6 to evacuate 2 men for "debility".	
"	26.2.17		Enquired 104th Fd. Ambce at CAYEUX. Demand under shelter; ammunition & approach deep in mud. " 107th Fd. Ambulance ammunits. Stabled in barn; ammunition sorties flooding.	
"	27.2.17		Conferred with Dumas with 157 & 159 Bdes. Casualties normal & doing satisfactorily. Treatment of cases difficult under present muddy condition of stationing.	
"	28.2.17		Attended Conference at AH. 25, 4th Army.	

M.N.Taylor, Major, A.M.C.
A.D.V.S. 35th Div.

Army Form C. 2118.

WAR DIARY of A.D.V.S. 35th Div.
or
INTELLIGENCE SUMMARY.
(Erase heading not required.)

Vol 14

Instructions regarding War Diaries and Intelligence Summaries are contained in F. S. Regs., Part II. and the Staff Manual respectively. Title pages will be prepared in manuscript.

Place	Date	Hour	Summary of Events and Information	Remarks and references to Appendices
G.H.Q.	1.3.17		Reported Horses at 105th & 106th Infantry Bde. Hd. Qrs. Condition rather [illeg.] Met [illeg.] of 201st F.C.R.E. at PREUX. Condition fairly good.	
	2.3.17		Inspected Horses of III Corps Reposte at LATTRE. Condition rather [illeg.]. Wrote reference to V.G.n. at my office.	
	3.3.17		Inspected M. 1, 2, 3 & 4 Co. Divisional Train. Animals are found worked to death & mange having every to the three heavy horses has been evacuated, but are recovering. A male [illeg.] horses on each company in light condition & recommended rest.	
	4.3.17		Inspected C. 124th Horses 157th F.A.Bde. Condition generally [illeg.] satisfactory. About 14 horses in light condition.	
	5.3.17		Inspected A & B Battery Horses 157th F.A. Bde. "A" Battery horses in fair condition; about 9 horses in light condition. "B" " " generally good condition.	

Army Form C. 2118.

WAR DIARY
or
INTELLIGENCE SUMMARY.
(Erase heading not required.)

Place	Date	Hour	Summary of Events and Information	Remarks and references to Appendices
CRIX	6.3.17		Reported 13 Battery ?????? 159" F.A. Brig. Ammunition dump ? Philston ????.	
"	7.3.17		Reported A & B ?????? 159" F.A. Brig. Ammunition dump in full batteries park. Ammunition ??????.	
"	8.3.17		Reported C & D Battery ?????? 159" F.A. Brig. Ammunition under front ???; Small percentage in light ammunition.	
"	9.3.17		Reported ?????? at M.V.A. for ammunition to ?????? " " 256" Tunnelling Co R.E. Evacuated 1 N.D. with ?????? to M.V.A. Reported 2 ????? ?? amphibitus ammunition.	
"	10.3.17		Reported 105" F. Amb ?????? Ammunition ?????? dump. Park Mules ? 104" & 105" btys Photos ? ammunition under ??????	

Army Form C. 2118.

WAR DIARY
or
INTELLIGENCE SUMMARY.
(Erase heading not required.)

Instructions regarding War Diaries and Intelligence Summaries are contained in F. S. Regs., Part II. and the Staff Manual respectively. Title pages will be prepared in manuscript.

Place	Date	Hour	Summary of Events and Information	Remarks and references to Appendices
C.A. X	11.3.17		Inspected 104" Bty Pcks & M.T. &c. Enrolls of 10.2.4. Mules from Otter Oper. into [illegible].	
"	12.3.17		Inspected Horses Mules in 35" D.A.C. No. 1 Section Reward/[illegible] 1 about 10/ horses in [illegible] condition. " 2 " Good condition " 18/3 " " " " 3 " Mules in good condition. Wrote on [illegible] horse & pony very [illegible].	
"	13.3.17		Inspected 105" Bty Pcks horses & mules. 15" Ukrainian [illegible] [illegible] [illegible] [illegible] fair response however [illegible] from 16 " " 14 Ukrainian " 15 Ukrainian " 10.5 M.T. Co. [illegible] fair to [illegible] on the light on [illegible]	

WAR DIARY
or
INTELLIGENCE SUMMARY.
(Erase heading not required.)

Army Form C. 2118.

Place	Date	Hour	Summary of Events and Information	Remarks and references to Appendices
CA/X	14.3.17		Reports make them on N.V.A. for ammunition.	
			35" D.W.G. Pieces 9 rounds at Bank station	
			Conditions fair : 3 hours in flight condition.	
"	15.3.17		Reports 106" Hy. Bty. R.G.	
			17" Carpt Line 6 : Condition fair ; Made in flight condition .	
			19" D " " " good.	
			18" N " " " fair.	
			17" West " " " good.	
			" 106" M. G. L. " good.	
"	16.3.17		Reports 203" H.L.R.E.	
			Condition 9 rounds anti-aircraft.	
			" 204" " " R.E.	
			Condition anti-aircraft.	
			" 205" " 6 R.E.	
			Condition fair : Want of ammunition + V.G.	

WAR DIARY
or
INTELLIGENCE SUMMARY.

(Erase heading not required.)

Army Form C. 2118.

Instructions regarding War Diaries and Intelligence Summaries are contained in F.S. Regs., Part II. and the Staff Manual respectively. Title pages will be prepared in manuscript.

Place	Date	Hour	Summary of Events and Information	Remarks and references to Appendices
CAIX	17.3.17		Reports to 106 F. Ambulance convoy. Condition very poor.	
ROSIERES	19.3.17		Moved to ROSIERES in charge of No. 1 D.R.S.	
"	19.3.17		Attended a Conference at 4th Army No. 2 D.R.	
"	20.3.17 to 25.3.17		Reported sick. Sent home to England. G.C. A.S.M.R.1 acting A.D.V.1.	
"	26.3.17		Returned from leave & resumed duty.	
"	27.3.17		Inspected cases at No. 1 D.R.S. for evacuation to England.	

Army Form C. 2118.

WAR DIARY
or
INTELLIGENCE SUMMARY.
(Erase heading not required.)

Instructions regarding War Diaries and Intelligence Summaries are contained in F. S. Regs., Part II. and the Staff Manual respectively. Title pages will be prepared in manuscript.

Place	Date	Hour	Summary of Events and Information	Remarks and references to Appendices
ROSIERES	28.9.17		Rifuts attempt moved to 15 Division. Consists of Mules, forms, Drawn Gun transport. Arrived 35 R.A. that L.D. Artillery horses are allowed 2½ oz water oats	
NESLE	29.9.17		Imputs 105 P. Antichan. Inoculated 1 N.P & M.V.A. Condition note fratery. "18" L.Y. "18" M.S.Co. Cart the Bar. has injured. Moved to NESLE on Strength of D.M.P.	
"	30.9.17		Imputs 106 Y. Antichan Condition notes fratery. "104" M.S.Co. Condition of animals notes fratery. N.V.A. in new billet at OILLANCOURT Accommodation good.	
			Horses off in new order month that with remounts. Woke comty horses; A few left in lort.	

A5834 Wt.W4973/M687 750,000 8/16 D.D.&L. Ltd. Forms/C.2118/13.

WAR DIARY
INTELLIGENCE SUMMARY

Army Form C. 2118.

Place	Date	Hour	Summary of Events and Information	Remarks and references to Appendices
NESLE	21.9.17		Infants 19 M the hospital. Conditions poor. detached 107 F. Amb. at HERLY. Conditions noted findings. 14 Slomenden. Conditions poor, of good; 3 L.D. horses in light condition; equipt minimal. detachment of N°1, & 2 sections D.M.C. Condition fine. Relations from various. 2.4.17	

W.N. Taylor. Major. A.V.C.
19.V.1 35" Div.

Army Form C. 2118.

WAR DIARY of A.D.V.S. 35th Div.
or
INTELLIGENCE SUMMARY.
(Erase heading not required.)

Place	Date	Hour	Summary of Events and Information	Remarks and references to Appendices
NESLE	1.4.17		Inspected horses for evacuation at M.V.T.	
			16th Divl Train transport. Condition of animals notin frosting.	
			17th West Yorks. Animals in fair condition.	
			19th D.I.T.T. Condition of animals satisfactory.	
	2.4.17		No. 2 C. A.T.C. Condition of animals passed good.	
			204th F.C. R.E. Condition satisfactory.	
	3.4.17		No. 2 Section D.A.C. Condition fair: Animals in light condition.	
	4.4.17		Weather conditions still bad. Snow falling most of the day. Inspected animals arrived at M.V.T. Detachment of M.V.T. proceeded to VOYENNES.	

WAR DIARY
or
INTELLIGENCE SUMMARY.

(Erase heading not required.)

Army Form C. 2118.

Instructions regarding War Diaries and Intelligence Summaries are contained in F. S. Regs., Part II. and the Staff Manual respectively. Title pages will be prepared in manuscript.

Place	Date	Hour	Summary of Events and Information	Remarks and references to Appendices
WESLE	5.4.17		Impeta No. 1. C.A.V.C. Remounted I.N.D to M.V.1. Unable to convert Fawcett auto fasten.	
"	6.4.17		Impeta 159° 4.A.Bdr. A. Bty in form condition: B " " very poor C " " in many cases too light & requires a rest. D " " Fair. A rest-ration horses more in light condition	
	7.4.17		Impeta rode around on Mobile Veterinary Section	
	8.4.17		Impeta 159° 4.A.12 Bdr. A. Bty about 16 animals in light condition others generally in to fair cond. Animals V.6 to remain to 5 rehabilitate animals. B. Bty. Unlike good. C " " fair D " " generally poor.	
	9.4.17		Mobile Vet. Section arrived to BUNY.	

Army Form C. 2118.

WAR DIARY
or
INTELLIGENCE SUMMARY.
(Erase heading not required.)

Instructions regarding War Diaries and Intelligence Summaries are contained in F. S. Regs., Part II. and the Staff Manual respectively. Title pages will be prepared in manuscript.

Place	Date	Hour	Summary of Events and Information	Remarks and references to Appendices
NESLE	10.4.17		Reports M.V.1 at BUNY. Accommodation for horses being found. "109" F. Ambulance Cavalry to remain front. Reinforcement 1. L.D. belongs to 168° F.A. Bde. 32° Div. in all-front condition.	
"	11.4.17		M.V.1 moved to Y.	
MONCHY-LAGACHE	12.4.17		Reported with unit for inspection at M.V.1. March to MONCHY-LAGACHE.	
"	13.4.17		Reports horses to hospital & R.A. Hd. 25. Cavalry friendly front. M.V.1 moved to GUIZANCOURT. Weekly conference at V.G.	
"	14.4.17		Reports 104° Bgn. Rds. condition. 19° I. Ygs. " " 16° I. Ygs " L.D. Mulcher, another spare, Other animals fair. 20° I. Ygs " condition under treatment. 33° Manchester " " Horses on front road - from to day.	

WAR DIARY
or
INTELLIGENCE SUMMARY.

(Erase heading not required.)

Army Form C. 2118.

Place	Date	Hour	Summary of Events and Information	Remarks and references to Appendices
MONCHY-LAGACHE	15-4-17		Prefects known to ISG" F.A. Bde.:- A. Bty condition fair; improving. B. " " going forward. C. " " fair; horses much improved. D. " " ; one sub-section in light condition.	
"	16-4-17		35° Div: Roads about Roisel & onwards condition fair. No.1 Auxilia. 35" D.A.C. condition antis forward. No.1 Co. 1.A.T.C. condition poor. No.4 Co. 1.A.T.C. Condition of animals any poor.	
"	17-4-17		35° Imped to Roisel area. Complete to Roisel front. 2°&3° F.C. R.E. condition antis forward: Order published in D.R.O., no change from previous.	

Army Form C. 2118.

WAR DIARY
or
INTELLIGENCE SUMMARY.
(Erase heading not required.)

Instructions regarding War Diaries and Intelligence Summaries are contained in F. S. Regs., Part II. and the Staff Manual respectively. Title pages will be prepared in manuscript.

Place	Date	Hour	Summary of Events and Information	Remarks and references to Appendices
MIRCHY-LAGACHE	18.4.17		Infantry M.V.1 at MERAUCOURT. Ammunition park.	
"	19.4.17		Reports Nos 2 & 3 Ln. A.A.C. Ammunition anti-feeling " 106 Fd Ambulance Ammunition park.	
"	20.4.17		Monthly conference of V.G. Detachment of M.V.1 proceeds to VILLEVEQUE.	
"	21.4.17		Reports following units with D.A.Q.M.G. " 18th L.F.A. Ammunition-ammunition; 6.8 mules on light ammunition. " 17th L.F. Ammunition park. " 106 M.F.G. Ammunition any park.	
"	22.4.17		Inspects 107 Fd Ambulance Ammunition & mounds any park.	

A5834 Wt W4973/M657 750,000 8/16 D. D. & L. Ltd. Forms/C.2118/13.

Army Form C. 2118.

WAR DIARY
or
INTELLIGENCE SUMMARY.
(Erase heading not required.)

(6)

Instructions regarding War Diaries and Intelligence Summaries are contained in F.S. Regs., Part II. and the Staff Manual respectively. Title pages will be prepared in manuscript.

Place	Date	Hour	Summary of Events and Information	Remarks and references to Appendices
MONCHY-LAGACHE	23.4.17		Reports 106° M.G.C. Condition of ammunition good. Instructed O.C. H.S. M.G.C. to send 1 Corporal + 3 men A.V.C. to report to V.6.4. to Corps transport for duty.	
"	24.4.17		Reports 105° Batty. Below 104. 2/c ; Condition of ammunition good. 15° Wilshire " " partially " 16 " " " 14° Blenratt " " " 15° Watts, Derby " " " 105° M.G.C. " " good ; Ammo. first ten long. Inspected Waltham, Peter 13m.tm, Benton, & Vauxhauser sent to IV Corps.	
"	25.4.17		Reports 19° Bn. D.I.I. Condition of ammunition good. 17° M.r. Punjab Rifles Condition good.	

WAR DIARY
or
INTELLIGENCE SUMMARY.

(Erase heading not required.)

Army Form C. 2118.

Place	Date	Hour	Summary of Events and Information	Remarks and references to Appendices
MONCHY - LA GACHE	26.4.17		Reports 17°/Apr. West Spurs. Demolition point. " 18° N.2.9 Demolition fired " 20.4.7. to R.E. Demolition very good.	
"	27.4.17		" 19°/Apr. Motherhead Providen. Demolition to succeed very good." Night conference to V.G.	
"	28.4.17		" 30 6° 7.A. 12h. (attached) A. Btry " Demolition Good " demo cover of hire " B " " " " 15% " height demolition " C " " " " 20% " " " D " " " " 20% " " "	

Army Form C. 2118.

WAR DIARY
or
INTELLIGENCE SUMMARY.

(Erase heading not required.)

Place	Date	Hour	Summary of Events and Information	Remarks and references to Appendices
RONCHY-LAGACHE	29/4/17		Reported 159° F.A. Robn. @ [illegible] firing proof. A Bty: Condition [illegible] in any good; then inspected. B " C " Found condition; then inspected. D " Firing proof.	
	30/4/17		Reported 105° F. Ambulance. Condition of ammunition fractured. I.N.B ammunition to N.W.A. " 205° F.W. R.E. Condition of ammunition antisatisfactory. Arrangements made to such ammunition transferred to Bouer for last 12 weeks is 10 rounds.	

W.N. Taylor, Major A.V.C.
A.D.V.S. 35° Div.

Army Form C. 2118.

WAR DIARY of ADVI. 35 Div
or
INTELLIGENCE SUMMARY.
(Erase heading not required.)

Place	Date	Hour	Summary of Events and Information	Remarks and references to Appendices
MONCHY — LAGACHE	1.5.17		Inspected No. 1. Station 35th R.A.C. Condition found good; Running with six Huts on 50% normal." " No. 3. Station " " Condition good.	
"	2.5.17		Inspected No. 2. Station 35th D.A.C. (attached 32nd Div D.A.C.) Condition found good; Casualties normal.	
	3.5.17		Attended conference at A.D.V.S. at Hd. 25th A. Army.	
	4.5.17		Made inference to V.G. at my Office. Inspected horses for evacuation at M.V.1.	
	5.5.17		Inspected following transport:— 16th Cheshires : Condition good. 107th F. Ambulance " " 23rd Manchesters " " Casualties normal. Attended demonstration at Div for School in firing Anti-fur Horse Respirators.	

Army Form C. 2118.

WAR DIARY
or
INTELLIGENCE SUMMARY.
(Erase heading not required.)

Instructions regarding War Diaries and Intelligence Summaries are contained in F. S. Regs., Part II. and the Staff Manual respectively. Title pages will be prepared in manuscript.

Place	Date	Hour	Summary of Events and Information	Remarks and references to Appendices
MONCHY-LAGACHE	6.5.17		Inspected men at M.V.S.1 for evacuation to Base.	
			18" Pounder Brigade. Condition improving	
"	7.5.17		157" F.A. Bde.	
			A Battery; Condition general good; 10% light condition	
			B " " Good "	
			C " " Good; Several cases of lice for treatment.	
			D " " generally good	
"	8.5.17		Inspected N.1. W. R.A.T.C.	
			Condition general good; Casualties normal.	
			19"/14pr Northumberland Fusiliers	
			Condition of animals very good.	
"	9.5.17		Inspected sick men at M.V.S.1 for evacuation to hospital.	
"	10.5.17		" 2 " W.R.T.C	
			" 3 " "	
			" 4 " "	
			Condition general good; Casualties normal.	

WAR DIARY
INTELLIGENCE SUMMARY.
(Erase heading not required.)

Army Form C. 2118.

Place	Date	Hour	Summary of Events and Information	Remarks and references to Appendices
DONCHY-LAGACHE	11.5.17		Weekly endorsement to V.C.	
"	12.5.17		19/181 Sergt. Murby A.V.C. transferred from H.S.M.V.A. to No. 2 section - 35' D.U.	
	13.5.17		Inspected 106.13th M.U. 26. Constitution of animals noted fractions. 18" Cat G. 1; Arms L.D. Mules in light condition. 17" Mule forks. Condition poor.	
	14.5.17		Inspected horses at M.C.A. for evacuation to Rouen.	
	15.5.17		Accompanied D.D.V.S. 4th Army on his inspection of IV Corps Heavy Artillery	
	16.5.17		Inspected 110 Remount detained in PERONNE. Condition generally good; dealing period animals appear to have travelled well.	

Army Form C. 2118.

WAR DIARY
INTELLIGENCE SUMMARY.
(Erase heading not required.)

Instructions regarding War Diaries and Intelligence Summaries are contained in F. S. Regs., Part II. and the Staff Manual respectively. Title pages will be prepared in manuscript.

Place	Date	Hour	Summary of Events and Information	Remarks and references to Appendices
MONCHY-LAGACHE	17.5.17		Inspected 110 Remounts before issue to units of the Div. Found suffering from sore shoulders, sore girth & cutaneous irritation & contact urticata.	
"	18.5.17		Weekly conference of V.Os. Inspected horses for evacuation at M.V.S.	
"	19.5.17		Inspected 18th Tunnelling Coy horses. Condition & general management.	
"	20.5.17		Proceeded to PERONNE — change of D.D.V.S. Lieut Col R.W. D.V.S.	
"	21.5.17		Inspected 109th F. Ambulance. Condition horses. 204th F. Coy R.E. Condition army horses.	
"	22.5.17		10th Mtd Bde at PERONNE. Condition general good.	

Army Form C. 2118.

WAR DIARY
INTELLIGENCE SUMMARY.
(Erase heading not required.)

Instructions regarding War Diaries and Intelligence Summaries are contained in F. S. Regs., Part II. and the Staff Manual respectively. Title pages will be prepared in manuscript.

Place	Date	Hour	Summary of Events and Information	Remarks and references to Appendices
PERONNE	23.5.17		C/St. P.J. TURNER A.V.C. proceeded to 5th Div. for duty. Authority D.D.V.S. 4th Army. Am/plan to establishment of 35 Div. Inspected 45th M.V.S. at TEMPLEUX-LA-FOSSE.	
"	24.5.17		Inspected 105th Bdy, Bde + M.T.C. at PERONNE. Condition generally good. No. 3. W.V.S.C. Condition poor; Evacuate 3.N.D. to M.V.S for hospital. 203rd F.C. R.E. Condition fair; ought to be improved.	
GURLU-WOOD	25.5.17		Proceeded to GURLU-WOOD in charge of horses in 9PM. One horse + 3 men A.V.C. sent to XV Corps to form detachment M.V.S.	
"	26.5.17		Inspected 159th F.A. Bde lines at HEUDECOURT. Watering from troughs; small pond. 105th Inf. Bde lines; small pond. Watering from troughs; small pond. 104th + 106th Bdy Bde lines at HEUDECOURT. Watering from troughs; small pond. Asked TOWN-MAJOR to have up a town table for watering.	

A 5834 Wt. W4973/M687 750,000 8/16 D.D. & L. Ltd. Forms/C.2118/13.

Army Form C. 2118.

WAR DIARY
INTELLIGENCE SUMMARY
(Erase heading not required.)

Instructions regarding War Diaries and Intelligence Summaries are contained in F. S. Regs., Part II. and the Staff Manual respectively. Title pages will be prepared in manuscript.

Place	Date	Hour	Summary of Events and Information	Remarks and references to Appendices
GURLU-WOOD	29/5/17		Reported M.1 6 A.T.C.	
			" 2 "	
			" 3 "	
			" 4 "	
			Smiths pool : Casualties from : Walking from trench 2 M/M power	
	28/5/17		Reported 10.5" Rds N0.2.6 :	
			Smiths 6 passed anti-fouling : Some Mules not having feet.	
			" 15" Chatham	
			Casualties passed pond : A Coy 4.B Mules might be influenced.	
			Transports 1.6.B to M.v.T.	
			" 16" Chatham	
			Smiths pond	
			" 14" Shoreham	
			Smiths pond + Derby	
			15" MATS + Derby	
			Smiths pond : Transports 1.2.B Mules to hospital.	
	29/5/17		Reported 15.5 Heavy Btys on inclination from D.D.V.T.	
			Rebels 20 covers on inclination for stabilisers :- Transfer by Three of these were mutilated	
			to Manapla to H.N.D. + 1 Riders officer to be attached with Manapla.	

Army Form C. 2118.

WAR DIARY
INTELLIGENCE SUMMARY.
(Erase heading not required.)

Place	Date	Hour	Summary of Events and Information	Remarks and references to Appendices
GURLU-WOOD.	30/5/17		Parapets 106° Adjn. Rly.	
			141.25°: Crater pond.	
			" 19° 9. 2. 9. " Emmenated 1. N.B. with defensive burg.	
			" 18° N. 2. 9. " "	
			" 17° Royal Scots " "	
			" Emmenated 2. N.B. for cups & movement.	
			" 17° West front. "	
			" Crater pond.	
			" 106° M. 7. 6	
			" Crater pond.	
	31/5/17		Parapets 104° Adjn. Rly.	
			Rly 25°: Crater pond.	
			" 17° Inns. Hamilton "	
			" 18° " " Fair: happening	
			" 20° " " "	
			" 23° Manchester " "	
			" 104° M. 7. 6	
			" Crater way pond.	
			" 203° F. L. R.E.	
			Crater fine: Cup containing twin shed: Informed C.6 that these timer is minimum	

W.H. Taylor Major
A.D.V.S. 35° Div

Army Form C. 2118.

WAR DIARY of D.A.D.V.S. 35th Div.
or
INTELLIGENCE SUMMARY.
(Erase heading not required.)

Instructions regarding War Diaries and Intelligence Summaries are contained in F. S. Regs., Part II. and the Staff Manual respectively. Title pages will be prepared in manuscript.

Place	Date	Hour	Summary of Events and Information	Remarks and references to Appendices
CURLU-WOOD	1.6.17		Inspected 157th F.A. Bde. Condition generally good. Evacuate two horses for Anaple + Worn out. No.1 Section D.A.C. Condition good. Watchf improvement of V.G.	
	2.6.17		Inspected No. 2 Section 35th D.A.C. Condition generally good. Evacuate three horses tired from later work. Details No.1 Section D.A.C. Condition good; spare animals somewhat light condition. No. 3. Section D.A.C. Condition generally good. 107th F. Ambulance; Condition good. Evacuate 1 (N.D) with Chronic Lymphitis. Veterinary equipment complete.	
	3.6.17		Inspected 105th F. Ambulance. Condition good. 106th F. Ambulance. Condition good. 205th Fd. Coy. R.E. Condition generally good.	

A5834 Wt W4973/M687 750,000 8/16 D. D. & L. Ltd. Forms/C.2118/13.

Army Form C. 2118.

WAR DIARY
or
INTELLIGENCE SUMMARY.
(Erase heading not required.)

Place	Date	Hour	Summary of Events and Information	Remarks and references to Appendices
GURLU-WOOD	4.6.17		Inspected 159" F. A. Bde.	
			A Bty. Excellent park	
			B " "	
			C " ammunition dugout; about 24 Rounds too deep; preventing easy reach	
			D " " park	
			Inspected for 3 unit checks for Bde.	
			Inspected 19" North. Fusiliers Veterinary equipment pack.	
			Condition very good.	
			" 204" F. C. R.E.	
			Condition very good.	
	5.8.17		Took report to D.D.V.S. Army on ammunition quantities of Mule teams.	
			Reported on run to the Plate, on formation of R.V.M.	
			Material stored. Enrolled in any remarkable factory.	
			Took sample of Plate sword to D.D.V.S. Army.	

Army Form C. 2118.

WAR DIARY
or
INTELLIGENCE SUMMARY.
(Erase heading not required.)

Instructions regarding War Diaries and Intelligence Summaries are contained in F. S. Regs., Part II. and the Staff Manual respectively. Title pages will be prepared in manuscript.

Place	Date	Hour	Summary of Events and Information	Remarks and references to Appendices
CURLU-WOOD	6.6.17		Met D.D.R of appointment at 4S MVI for entering of remount depots, went & sent to them for disposal.	
"	7.6.17		Inspected 203rd L.R.E. Armed men inoculated & training duty	
"	8.6.17		Visited informers & V.Ss.	
"	9.6.17		Inspected units of 106 Bty. R.F.A. Convalescent horses to dumping under feeding, unit of 106 M.G.Co. Convalescent horses & dumping under feeding	
"	10.6.17		Inspected sick cases at M.V.A. for examination to hospital	
"	11.6.17		Inspected units of 104 Bty. R.F.A. Convalescent animals to dumping under treatment. Evacuated 3 animals from 104 L.P. to M.V.A.	

Army Form C. 2118.

WAR DIARY
or
INTELLIGENCE SUMMARY.
(Erase heading not required.)

Place	Date	Hour	Summary of Events and Information	Remarks and references to Appendices
GURLU-WOOD	12.6.17		Inspected cart animal of 35' D.A.C. Few casualties; doing well.	
"	13.6.17		Inspected sick of 157' F.A. Bde. Casualties normal. Front cover of Ophthalmic on each battery platform for travel on the lorries. No.1. Section 35' D.A.C. Casualties few; health and condition good.	
"	14.6.17		Inspected 105' Fd. Amb'lance. Condition veterinary equipment good. " 205 " " " " R.E. Condition good. " 106 " Fd. Ambulance. Condition very good; harness. Ind. A.D. Mules 15 M.V.S.	
"	15.6.17		Inspected Veterinary Equipment of 35' Div. Train. No. 1 Co. Begun to be Veterinary table. Personnel an new State. " 2 " " " " " " " " 3 " " " " + one from 6 Divisions Remount submitted.	

Army Form C. 2118.

WAR DIARY
or
INTELLIGENCE SUMMARY.
(Erase heading not required.)

Instructions regarding War Diaries and Intelligence Summaries are contained in F. S. Regs., Part II. and the Staff Manual respectively. Title pages will be prepared in manuscript.

Place	Date	Hour	Summary of Events and Information	Remarks and references to Appendices
GOREV-WOOD	16.6.17		Inspected the rooms for ammunition in 159th Bde. 182th ammunition to M.G.C.	
"	17.6.17		Inspected with Emm at M.G.C. for ammunition to Brigades	
"	18.6.17		Inspected 106" Bdy. Bdes to 106 M.G.C. bullets proved correct from fuse they on 106 M.M.G.C.	
"	19.6.17		Inspected 203rd Co. R.E. New mutations at SERAMONT. Amtitte form. Bennmount Immediately 10th STOCKWELL & WOODCOCK to instruct instrument to complete intelligence of M.M.G.	
"	20.6.17		Attended F.G.C.M. to give evidence as to efficiency of S.A.A. Ufr. M.n.6 A.S.C.	
"	21.6.17		Inspected 19th Northumberland Fusiliers Ammunition lores 14th Northumberland Condition pres 15th Notts & Derby Ammunition pres	

Army Form C. 2118.

WAR DIARY
or
INTELLIGENCE SUMMARY.
(Erase heading not required.)

Instructions regarding War Diaries and Intelligence Summaries are contained in F. S. Regs., Part II. and the Staff Manual respectively. Title pages will be prepared in manuscript.

Place	Date	Hour	Summary of Events and Information	Remarks and references to Appendices
ROEUX- WOOD	22.6.17		Inspected 16" Chubosier. Bombarded 1.6.D. with "Buster Wood"; Pople 1.6.D. to 11.1.7 for shipping for chin operations. Condition generally poor. " 15" Chubosier. Bombarded 1.6.D. Made top shrine bombardment battles from . might the supervise. " 10.5" M.I.E. Bombarded 1.6.D. with fire table of Polaining Brook.	
"	23.6.17		Inspected and room of 35" D.N. C. Ammunition Room & during auto firing.	
"	24.6.17		Witnessed stat- A.D.V.S. men at Hpuchu at VII Corps, that will return from to be forwarded to Corps.	
"	25.6.17		Inspected and of 159" F.A. Robes Ammunition quoud & doing auto firing. 18" N.T. Condition good. Ammunition good. Inspected top can of other effection reported 7 V.G. ; have do not 3 hours to the company.	

Army Form C. 2118.

WAR DIARY
or
INTELLIGENCE SUMMARY.
(Erase heading not required.)

Place	Date	Hour	Summary of Events and Information	Remarks and references to Appendices
GURLU-WOOD	26.6.17		Inspected cars of 107 F. Ambulance. Casualties normal. " 16' Clearing casualties satisfactory; casualties normal.	
"	27.6.17		Inspected 17' Corps Posts. Casualties ample; conditions generally good. " 17 West Parks. Casualties normal; conditions good. Visited D.A.D.M.S and the question of watering troops would be more improved though from Commandants.	
"	28.6.17		Inspected all horses mechanist at 45' M.V.1. No veterinar.	
"	29.6.17		Inspected 50 Remounts at D.A.S.G. Lines received from ABBEVILLE. All other free from them diseases.	
"	30.6.17		Capt. W. B. De Venis A.V.C. (O.C. 45 M.V.1) proceeded to 16' Divn. to take up appointment of D.A.D.V.1 (Instruction from III Corps dated 29.6.17). Capt. H.J. LOWE A.V.C. to take over his duties on return from leave.	W.N. Joughin, Major. A.V.C. D.A.D.V.1. 35 Days.

WAR DIARY of D.A.D.V.S. 35" Div.

Army Form C. 2118.

INTELLIGENCE SUMMARY.

(Erase heading not required.)

Place	Date	Hour	Summary of Events and Information	Remarks and references to Appendices
GURLU-WOOD	1.7.17		Infantry 84 Remounts arrived from ABBEVILLE. Animals appeared in fair condition & free from contagious diseases; though age somewhat high.	
	2.7.17		Inspected cows for evacuation at Mobile Veterinary Section. Instructed Capt. P.J. White to take over the 45 M.V.S.	
	3.7.17		Evacuated 6 horses to M.V. Hospital from TINCOURT	
	4.7.17		Left R.J. Horse A.V.C. reported from leave to England. Instructions issued to Lieut. N.L. Pearson to be attached to 19" A.S. Rhu & to be in charge of the Hospital.	
	5.7.17		Proceeded on 14 days special leave to ENGLAND. Capt. J.J. Martin A.V.C. to do duty.	
	6.7.17		Inspected sick horses of 35 9 A.C. Casualties normal.	

Army Form C. 2118.

WAR DIARY
or
INTELLIGENCE SUMMARY.
(Erase heading not required.)

Instructions regarding War Diaries and Intelligence Summaries are contained in F. S. Regs., Part II. and the Staff Manual respectively. Title pages will be prepared in manuscript.

Place	Date	Hour	Summary of Events and Information	Remarks and references to Appendices
VILLERS-FAUCON	8.7.17		Attended a conference of Div. S.A.A. at 3rd Corps Hdqrs. Nest 25.	
"	8.7.17		Inspected chargers of 35° D.A.C. at a number of horses about 3/4 on light condition, & Inchitete on a horse brought for special attention.	
VILLERS-FAUCON	9.7.17		Proceeded to VILLERS-FAUCON in charge of D.A.D.V. 45 M.V.I moved to VILLERS-FAUCON.	
"	10.7.17		Inspected 107 F.A.Bde. Condition very good.	
"	11.7.17		35° Div. Amm. Col. Condition of animals very satisfactory.	
"	12.7.17		Inspected all equipment on charge of 45 M.V.I. & found all complete.	

A 5834 Wt.W4973/M687 750,000 8/16 D. D. & L. Ltd. Forms/C.2118/13.

WAR DIARY or INTELLIGENCE SUMMARY.

Army Form C. 2118.

(Erase heading not required.)

Instructions regarding War Diaries and Intelligence Summaries are contained in F. S. Regs., Part II. and the Staff Manual respectively. Title pages will be prepared in manuscript.

Place	Date	Hour	Summary of Events and Information	Remarks and references to Appendices
VILLERS BRETON	13/9/17		Inspected arrival at "45" M.A.C. for evacuation to Rouen.	
"	14/9/17		Attended conference of D.A.D.M.S. at 3rd Corps Head Quarters. Evacuated 8 women to Rouen Hospital.	
"	15/9/17		Inspected personnel of "45" M.V.S. in marching order.	
"	16/9/17		Visited conference at Divisional H.Q.	
"	17/9/17		Inspected arrival to hospital 6. + 109. F. Ambulance. Casualties few.	
"	18/9/17		Inspected arrival of "35" D.A.C. Casualties moved to Army anti-fretting.	

Army Form C. 2118.

WAR DIARY
or
INTELLIGENCE SUMMARY.
(Erase heading not required.)

Instructions regarding War Diaries and Intelligence Summaries are contained in F. S. Regs., Part II. and the Staff Manual respectively. Title pages will be prepared in manuscript.

Place	Date	Hour	Summary of Events and Information	Remarks and references to Appendices
VILLERS-FAUCON	19/7/17		Complete movement before move to unit (139). Conditions generally good. A first rainy check apparently spirit recovered from when trouble, but appears to be more general.	
"	20/7/17		Returned from leave to ENGLAND & reported around for am to A.D.V.S. III Corps. Complete movement of unit to Infantry unit, into 9.10 q.m.] H.Q. M.M.P. at VILLERS. FAUCON. Accommodation for horses good.	
"	21/7/17		Inspected 159' Bty. F.A. Bde. A 12 & D Batteries proved good. C Battery horses unsuitable than dulling (full anaemia) " 106 Hotch. Rkr & M.G.C. Conditions generally good ; must be seen first to be noted. " 205' Field Co. R.E. Conditions good ; horses first class.	

Army Form C. 2118.

WAR DIARY
or
INTELLIGENCE SUMMARY.

(Erase heading not required.)

Instructions regarding War Diaries and Intelligence Summaries are contained in F. S. Regs., Part II. and the Staff Manual respectively. Title pages will be prepared in manuscript.

Place	Date	Hour	Summary of Events and Information	Remarks and references to Appendices
VILLERS-FAUCON	22/7/17		Inspected 203rd E.C.R.E. Condition has recently improved: now general good.	
			" 204th F.C.R.E. Condition good.	
			" 19th Northumberland Fusiliers. Condition good.	
	23/7/17		" 157th F.A. Posts. Condition of horses general good. Some cases of footnote in much bothering. Curries protected to avoid sunburnt.	
		10 A.M.	Rifle Bgn. Posts. Horses Generally good.	
		10:30 M.G. Co.		
			Condition very good: Lieut. J.J. Hurdin R.V.C. granted leave to England from 25 Jnst to 2 August.	

WAR DIARY
or
INTELLIGENCE SUMMARY.

(Erase heading not required.)

Army Form C. 2118.

Place	Date	Hour	Summary of Events and Information	Remarks and references to Appendices
VILLERS-FAUCON	24/7/17		Computed 10.6 % Vaseline bulk powder. 10.6 % Anthracene bulk [illeg] gun powder. No. 1 Fraction 25 D.A.C. Combustion general good, some fumes on ignition, smoke blue (about 6½") No. 2 Fraction. Combustion general good; about 5 ft on height smoke blue. No. 3 Fraction. [illeg] general good.	
"	25/7/17		Computed 10.7 % Fraction. Combustion good. 25 Fraction ?. Combustion good. 10.5 % [illeg] Rifle + M.G. Combustion general good. 2 H.E.M.I.C. Combustion good.	

Army Form C. 2118.

WAR DIARY
or
INTELLIGENCE SUMMARY.
(Erase heading not required.)

Instructions regarding War Diaries and Intelligence Summaries are contained in F. S. Regs., Part II. and the Staff Manual respectively. Title pages will be prepared in manuscript.

Place	Date	Hour	Summary of Events and Information	Remarks and references to Appendices
VILLERS-FAUCON	26.7.17		Bombard B/210 12f. R.P.A meets Machine Gun Section. "A" subsection with 6.25" D.A.C. have antiaircraft.	
	27.7.17		Computed 3.5" Dis. Horses. Conducted any point; learned two guns.	
	28.7.17		Computed with horses for ammunition to France. 21 men commenced to prepare.	
	29.7.17		Computed three horses with 16 Chasseurs with others leaving & relieving made turnout. "A" Sub Battery with 15" Mrt's & Body munitions for return horses. horses coffers to be during action protect.	
	30.7.17		Computed and horses with 25" D.A.C. General terrain quiet B.C. 25" D.A.C. & antiaircraft men to duty. "B" Horses on three horses Conditio antiaircraft.	
	31.7.17		Computed with 16 10H Infy. Bde. Emerging and moved; horses with whom horses on 16 Chahi. hondols & rests for. with gun horses	W.M. Murphy Major RHA O.C. D/V.F. 3.6. Div.

Army Form C. 2118.

WAR DIARY of D.A.D.V.S. 35 Div
or
INTELLIGENCE SUMMARY.
(Erase heading not required.)

D.A.D.V.S.
35TH DIVISION.
No. 371
Date 1/9/17

Place	Date	Hour	Summary of Events and Information	Remarks and references to Appendices
VILLERS-FAUCON	1.8.17		Inspected 105th F. Ambulance: Condition of horses & mules very good. " sick animals for evacuation at 1st H.S. M.V.I.	
"	2.8.17		Inspected 35th Div. Supply Co. Condition of animals good: horses very reset. " 127th F. Ambulance. Condition very good.	
"	3.8.17		Inspected sick at M.V.1. for evacuation to hospital. " 241st M.T.C. Condition of animals good: horses seeing saddling.	
"	4.8.17		Evacuated 8 sick horses to 35th D.A.C. Inspected sick of 35th D.A.C. Casualties normal & evacuated enteric factory.	
"	5.8.17		Inspected Det. No.1. Divisn. 42nd D.A.C. Condition generally good.	
"	6.8.17		Mallesined 149 animals, 9 horses of 241st M.T. Co. R.E.	
"	7.8.17		Inspected animals of 241st M.T. Co.: No casualties. " 203rd 204th & 205th Field Co. R.E. Condition generally good: few casualties.	

WAR DIARY
or
INTELLIGENCE SUMMARY.

Army Form C. 2118.

Place	Date	Hour	Summary of Events and Information	Remarks and references to Appendices
WALKERS-FAUCON	8.8.17		Inspected mules of 106" Infy Bde. Casualties personnel nil. Mules of Sikhs & Lucknow Bde & mixed park. Few casualties.	
"	9.8.17		Inspected mules of 159" F.A. Bde. Present cases of Ophthalmia on each battery; otherwise evacuation normal.	
"	10.8.17		Inspected 19" W. Punjabis. Condition good. 105 V. Anderson. One case (remount) sent to M.V.S. suspected description mange.	
"	11.8.17		Inspected 4/6" F.A. Bde. (attached) Condition journey good. Recommended 2 cd. horses rested rather than for a fortnight & each of 36 horses.	
"	12.8.17		Inspected mules of Sikhs & Lucknow Bn. 114. 12. M. J. Syk. Condition good & treatment rather freeing.	

WAR DIARY
or
INTELLIGENCE SUMMARY.

Army Form C. 2118.

(Erase heading not required.)

Place	Date	Hour	Summary of Events and Information	Remarks and references to Appendices
VILLERS-FAUCON	13.9.17		Inspected units around by 35th D.M.C. A few cases of Ophthalmia; otherwise casualties normal. Horses for evacuation at 45th M.V.T.	
"	14.9.17		157 F.A. Bde. — 9, 13 — condition good — general good — C " " " " P " " good; improving hopping — Ground run to Ophthalmia in each Battery; horses isolated. Inspected 35 D A.C. No.1 Section — condition fair; two horses light about 10% " 2 " " " " " " " 3 " " general good.	
"	15.9.17		Inspected 159 F.A. Bde. Mares for breeding purposes on information from 3rd Corps.	
"	16.9.17		Attended as a Member of a Board re men through oats. Mathewsion of G.C.S. Younger on transfer to England.	

Army Form C. 2118.

WAR DIARY
or
INTELLIGENCE SUMMARY.
(Erase heading not required.)

Instructions regarding War Diaries and Intelligence Summaries are contained in F. S. Regs., Part II. and the Staff Manual respectively. Title pages will be prepared in manuscript.

Place	Date	Hour	Summary of Events and Information	Remarks and references to Appendices
NKHERS - FAYUM	17.9.17		Computed 157th F.A. Pack mounts & selected stores for breaking purposes	
"	18.9.17		Computed all Mares in 25th D.A.C. for breaking purposes. Attached in batymen of R.w.D., V.A. at 3=30pm.	
"	19.9.17		Selected mares for breaking purposes from 396th F.A. Pack.	
"	20.9.17		Computed mares of Field Ambulance, R.E., Infantry, M.G.Co, Pioneers, Supplies, Gunner + B.H.Q. Capt N.J. Lawson A.V.C. late 157 F.A. Pack reports to have been detached to C.C.A on 19th ult sent from here instead.	
"	21.9.17		Computed C + D Batteries 159 F.A. Pack. C. Bty horses half groomed. Saddles green. D Btry present period.	
"	22.9.17		Computed 155 Bty, 146th, 125 Mtn file. Saddles passed good. No Alteration + 155 Mtn file. not progressing sufficiently	

WAR DIARY
or
INTELLIGENCE SUMMARY.

(Erase heading not required.)

Army Form C. 2118.

Place	Date	Hour	Summary of Events and Information	Remarks and references to Appendices
VILLERS FAUCON	23/8/17		Inspected 106" Coy Rolls & M.T. C. Indian funeral parade. Car waiting available.	
"	24/8/17		Report move relation Committee convened at noon of Divisions & Corps 246' Rds. attached. Attended the parade.	
"	25/8/17		Inspected new compose train of 15 DAC & 159 HN Bde at H.Q.R at M.O.N.T.	
"	26/8/17		Inspected 15H Coy Rds & M.T. Cs Indian funeral pyre. Conversation Group.	
"	27/8/17		Inspected 2 other cars at M.T. Pinehin. Connected en-route to M.T. an Inspected & Wrought M.E. W.B.V.1 3" bdr at A.S. MAV.1 about the inspection.	
"	28/8/17		Inspected 107 Kniptoelshires 109 % inspection 204 % % R.E. Cattle general fount. 157 Rds M.F.C funds. Your case of Uffelhulm & for funds of there on the function.	

Army Form C. 2118.

WAR DIARY
or
INTELLIGENCE SUMMARY.
(Erase heading not required.)

Instructions regarding War Diaries and Intelligence Summaries are contained in F.S. Regs., Part II. and the Staff Manual respectively. Title pages will be prepared in manuscript.

Place	Date	Hour	Summary of Events and Information	Remarks and references to Appendices
VILLERS-FAUCON	29/10/17		Inspected horses of 35" D.A.C. with O.C. + O.R.S.A. 15 1/2 horses in light condition. Recommended 5 to N.V.D for evacuation.	
"	30/10/17		31 surplus horses + evacuated 9 for evacuation. D.A.V.S. 7th Army inspected A.S.M.V.S. Inspected 115 4th Ambulance: condition good.	
"	31/10/17		Inspected surplus D.M.C. horses + selected them suitable for Infantry Brigade of Division	

W.N. Taylor Major. A.V.C.
D.A.D.V.S. 2e Div.

A 5834 Wt. W4973/M687 750,000 8/16 D. D. & L. Ltd. Form/C.2118/13.

WAR DIARY

Army Form C. 2118

INTELLIGENCE SUMMARY

(Erase heading not required.)

Place	Date	Hour	Summary of Events and Information	Remarks and references to Appendices
VILLERS-FAUCON	1.9.17		Inspected 106 Field Ambulance. Condition very good. 16 Officers & 15 NCOs & ORs sick. Condition good & few casualties. All arrived on full rations from to day.	
"	2.9.17		Inspected another B.M.C. horses opened 1 D&S & M.5 to infantry Units & the Division. Arrangement now make to 25 D.A.C & 159 Bde R.F.A & MD & 2 Coys.	
"	3.9.17		Inspected mks to 35 Divn horses. Casualties normal & treatment on to factory. 205 & 6 R.E. Condition of units good. 203 F.C. R.E. Condition good & good 25 signal Co. Condition good & Civilian pop. & Casualties normal.	
"	4.9.17		A.S.C. 3rd Corps inspected this following units 159 F.A. Bde. 25 D.A.C. Attaching the ammunition.	

WAR DIARY
INTELLIGENCE SUMMARY
(Erase heading not required.)

Army Form C. 2118

Place	Date	Hour	Summary of Events and Information	Remarks and references to Appendices
VILLERS-FAUCON	5.9.17		[illegible handwritten entry]	
	6.9.17		[illegible handwritten entry]	
	7.9.17		[illegible handwritten entry]	
	8.9.17		[illegible handwritten entry]	

WAR DIARY
or
INTELLIGENCE SUMMARY
(Erase heading not required.)

Army Form C. 2118

Place	Date	Hour	Summary of Events and Information	Remarks and references to Appendices
WARLUS? BAU CAMP	9.9.17		Route march with teams to 159 F.A. Bde. Consolidation remounts & horsebreak unit quartout. Capt. G.B. Hopper (A.V.C.)(T.F.) reported for duty & is attached to 159 F.A. Bde in place of Lt/Col N.J. Purvis evacuated sick.	
"	10.9.17		Evacuate unfit chargers being remounted f 36 Div Train. Sick horses from European Army remount station, made f 105 Bty F.A. Bde. Yokum annoucement	
"	11.9.17		Mec A.D.V.S. 3rd Corps at LIERAMONT to inspect 159 Bde + 9 A.C. mobile vet stn Pullers out satisfactory. Inspects 203rd F.L. R.E. Condition of remounts poor.	
"	12.9.17		Inspects 147 Northumberland Fusiliers. Condition quite satisfactory. 107 Field Ambulance condition very poor. 36 Div. Supply Column Condition poor.	

WAR DIARY
or
INTELLIGENCE SUMMARY

(Erase heading not required.)

Army Form C. 2118

Place	Date	Hour	Summary of Events and Information	Remarks and references to Appendices
VILLERS-FAUCON	13.9.17		Conference at V.G. Report sent to A.D.V.S. 35th Div. re km [illegible] of stones being moved to unit area [illegible]. (Wheat & Oats.)	
"	14.9.17		Inspected mules of 35th D.A.C. & 159th F.A. Bde. Condition & turnout satisfactory. Animals moved. Impossible about 30 cases of opthalmia [illegible] lymph return to V.G. M.O. 25 M.V.S. & demonstration to the method on [illegible] to beginners. Lecture at 13th [illegible] [illegible] on [illegible] to beginners.	
"	15.9.17		Attended [illegible] to 158 U.G. [illegible] of D.D.V.S. 3rd Army. A number of horses are [illegible] unsuitable for [illegible] [illegible] [illegible].	
"	16.9.17		Inspected C. 185, 159 F.A. 12 bn. Lentils Park. Horses have [illegible] to being [illegible] to [illegible]. [illegible] 35th D.A.C. & 159 F.A. Bde. [illegible] during route [illegible].	
"	17.9.17		Inspected 135th & 136th F. Ambulances. Condition of animals very [illegible]. 311th 12 [illegible], [illegible] [illegible] 6 C.R.E. Condition mules [illegible].	

WAR DIARY
or
INTELLIGENCE SUMMARY

(Erase heading not required.)

Army Form C. 2118

Place	Date	Hour	Summary of Events and Information	Remarks and references to Appendices
VILLERS-FAUCON	18.9.17		Inspected A.(?).D. Returns 159 F.A. Bde Entile generally in a unsatisfactory manner.	
"	19.9.17		Inspected nose horses of 35 D.A.C, 159 F.A. Bde Remounts 10 cmr hyprs D.A.C horses of condition 5 cmr hyprs 159 F.A. Bde.	
"	20.9.17		Inspected mule transp V.A.C. 157 F.A. Bde & Wheelers attendance Mules & attendance are rather good esp. & inspected & q	
"	21.9.17		Inspected 104 Infy Bde & 104 M.G.C Condition generally good. Animals are watered & treatment rules & watering.	
"	22.9.17		Visited horse disp at BEAUMETZ 100 horses of D.A.C. put through the bath.	
"	23.9.17		Inspected 241st M.G.C Condition poor " 75 Trench Mortar Co Condition poor.	

WAR DIARY
or
INTELLIGENCE SUMMARY

Army Form C. 2118

(Erase heading not required.)

Instructions regarding War Diaries and Intelligence Summaries are contained in F. S. Regs., Part II. and the Staff Manual respectively. Title Pages will be prepared in manuscript.

Place	Date	Hour	Summary of Events and Information	Remarks and references to Appendices
VILLERS- FAUCON	24.9.17		Attached infantry to 151st F.A. Bde. of A.D.V.S. 3rd Corps. Available 2 horse power.	
"	25.9.17		Transferred 159 F.A. Bde. Available horses.	
"	26.9.17		Transferred 151 F. Ambulance. Available horses & M.R.S. 20.5.9 & 20.4.9 L Available personnel power.	
"	27.9.17		" 105 Bty. Palm " " M.R.S. 7 L. Available personnel power. Recommends cart as ambulance (Jeeds)	
"	28.9.17		Transferred with the 106 Bty Petrol. Casualty Sp. annexed & transport auto funting. 19 N. Eg. Available auto funting	
"	29.9.17		Transferred with to 159 F.A. Bde. two not. Ca annex & two int auto funting	
"	30.9.17		Transferred with 35 D.M.C. & 159 F.A. Bde. Casualties annexed. D.A.D.V.S. 56 Divn arrived at H.Q M.V.S with review of Vethy cars.	Y.M.S. Lympho Mayor S.C.C. R.W.D.V.S. 35 Vnn

1875 Wt. W593/826 1,000,000 4/15 J.B.C. & A. A.D.S.S./Forms/C. 2118.

Army Form C. 2118

WAR DIARY of D.A.D.V.S. 35th Div.

INTELLIGENCE SUMMARY

(Erase heading not required.)

Instructions regarding War Diaries and Intelligence Summaries are contained in F. S. Regs., Part II. and the Staff Manual respectively. Title Pages. will be prepared in manuscript.

Vol 21

Place	Date	Hour	Summary of Events and Information	Remarks and references to Appendices
VILLERS FAUCON	1.10.17		Inspected and drew forage for remounts at 5" M.V.T. Conference at 3m Corps HQ. 2 hrs.	
"	2.10.17		Inspected the following Units:— 203rd F. Co. R.E.; Condition poor. 19th Northumberland Fusiliers; Condition poor.	
BUISANS	3.10.17		D.A.D. moves to BUISANS. 45" M.V.T. moves to BAPAUME.	
"	4.10.17		45" M.V.T. moves to AGNEZ-LES-DUISANS. Inspected 23" F.C. R.E. Condition good. No casualties on march.	
"	5.10.17		Inspected the following Units:— 17" Rymt. Parks; Condition [?] poor. 35" [?] to [?]; [?] poor. 2nd Rations W.3. D.A.C.; condition poor. [?] casualties on the march.	
"	6.10.17		Inspected following units:— No 3 Sub Group; Condition poor. 15" Div Supply " " D.R.S. state that all horses to be clipped trace high.	

Army Form C. 2118

WAR DIARY
or
INTELLIGENCE SUMMARY

(Erase heading not required.)

Instructions regarding War Diaries and Intelligence Summaries are contained in F. S. Regs., Part II. and the Staff Manual respectively. Title Pages will be prepared in manuscript.

Place	Date	Hour	Summary of Events and Information	Remarks and references to Appendices
DUISANS	7/10/17		Completed the following:— 17 Tunnel posts; Candles present good. Whalen fans installed. 2 & 3" C. R.E. Candles posts. 3 S. dugout C. "	
"	8/10/17		Completed H.S. M.V.F. at A.G.118 2-LES-DUISANS.	
"	9/10/17		Repairs following:— 107. Dugout shelter; Candles to summer's any good. 119. W. Fontaine " Power of Kind. Connington annual " 205. P. C. R.E. Candles posts, good.	
"	10/10/17		Completed following:— 10 S. M.V.L; Candles satisfactory. 16 Mr. Dynamiters " 2nd further DMC ett. " Gun mellite annual.	
"	11/10/17		Completed work of H.S. M.V.F. for ammunition to complete.	

1875 Wt. W593/826 1,000,000 4/15 J.B.C. & A. A.D.S.S./Forms/C. 2118.

WAR DIARY
or
INTELLIGENCE SUMMARY

(Erase heading not required.)

Army Form C. 2118

Place	Date	Hour	Summary of Events and Information	Remarks and references to Appendices
DUISANS	12.10.17		D.MMP moves to LEDERZEELE.	
LEDERZEELE	13.10.17		Inspected 35' Regnd Co. Inside any part. Horses in the open. Condition satisfactory. Transport in the open. D.MMP horses.	
LEDERZEELE	14.10.17		HS'M.M.T.R. Veterans at CASSEL & marched to LEDERZEELE. Inspected No. 3 Co. 35' Div. train. Condition very good. Took charge of D.MMP transport & motor convoy to PROVEN.	
"	15.10.17			
"	16.10.17		MMC D.V.S.& V.T. Gunner Div. & arranged for HS'M.V.T. to take over from them.	
J. CAMP INTERNATIONAL CORNER	17.10.17		Took charge of D.MMP transport to J. CAMP. Met no 9 V.T. XII Corps & arranged for new location for M.V.T. HS'M.V.T. marched from LEDERZEELE to J. CAMP.	

Army Form C. 2118

WAR DIARY
or
INTELLIGENCE SUMMARY
(Erase heading not required.)

Instructions regarding War Diaries and Intelligence Summaries are contained in F. S. Regs., Part II. and the Staff Manual respectively. Title Pages will be prepared in manuscript.

Place	Date	Hour	Summary of Events and Information	Remarks and references to Appendices
J. CAMP.	18.10.17		H.S. M.V.S. moves to A.18.B.D.8 (Sheet 20). & acts as V.C.C.T. in impure line the H.A.M.V.S. for XIV & XVIII Corps.	
"	19.10.17		Inspects following Units:- 20 S. & G.R.E. Condition generally good. 20 H. " " " " 20 S. " " " " Stables in the open: Ammunition moved; 2 Horse-lines in the open. " 10.5 M.T.C. Condition generally good. 2 Horse-lines in the open.	
"	20.10.17		Conference of D.A.D.V.S. at Corps Head Qrs. 2.pm.	
"	21.10.17		Inspects the following:- No 1. Section D.A.C. Condition generally good. " 2. " " " " " " " 3. " " " " " " All animals standing in the open.	

WAR DIARY
or
INTELLIGENCE SUMMARY

(Erase heading not required.)

Army Form C. 2118

Place	Date	Hour	Summary of Events and Information	Remarks and references to Appendices
J.C.A.N.P.	22.10.17		Reports the following rounds: 7H.25, 756 RHD Plds. Emulsion of unused power. 19" Royal Invert Emulsite power: Whole roy power. 19" 9.2" 1. Ditto " " 19" Westr Repton " " 15" 75 T.E. " " 106 M.T.L.E. Complete power. M.T.W on other spare other rounds abolition. " 60 h.E. N.T.C. Emulsion powd. Whole abolition.	
"	23.10.17		Reports 159, 9.45. Plds. Primed, abolishing for the spare. Spare magazine of emulsion power. Work amongst shown to trade transports & long known stores. Numbers of amounts below. Apolied off to the normal transfers. Emulsion of amounts known powd.	

WAR DIARY
or
INTELLIGENCE SUMMARY

(Erase heading not required.)

Army Form C. 2118

Place	Date	Hour	Summary of Events and Information	Remarks and references to Appendices
J CAMP.	24.10.17		Imputes 106 H.Q. Bde. Consists of amend present point. All units were sent in succession [illegible] to 15" & 16" Howitzers. Con. A.D. amounts for 16 Howitzers [illegible] Mountings. 10.5" M.H.J 6 [illegible] Consists of general point. All arrived in open.	
"	25.10.17		W.O.V.J. XII. Steps completed. Asst. the inspection. 4.5" M.H.J contained 267 rounds. Work tending to day 9.8 rounds submitted for Funds. Horse ammn, 32 shine & 6 shotgun.	
"	26.10.17		Imputes 107 B. [illegible] ammn made [illegible]. Cordite low-owing point. 18" Northumberland Fusiliers. Cordite present point. Arrived in the open.	
"	27.10.17		Imputes no 1 C, A.F.E. Arrived in open in good standing. Cordite point. 35" [illegible]. Ammns made platoon. Conference at B.H.Q. V.P. at 12.15.	

WAR DIARY
or
INTELLIGENCE SUMMARY

Army Form C. 2118

Place	Date	Hour	Summary of Events and Information	Remarks and references to Appendices
S. CAMP.	28/11/17		Infants Present at PROVEN STN. with DAQMS f.	
"	29/11/17		Infantry sick horses to 85 DAC. Truck morning under tour. Returns B No 1. Section monthly under war premiums on form 45. M.I.? remounts right annual.	
"	30/11/17		Infantry. 16 horses B M.S. to 60 D.C. remounted f. Presents. Mounts to 2n remounted to D.N.I. 33 Mules, O.R. No.3. Section D.19.C. Rifles v remounted f Armoury. 103 Inf Rifles v M.S.G. horses f. 20 v 18 D.A.C in bad condition, still amount on the form Inoculation f armoury pork.	
"	31/11/17		Infants 241 M.T.b. Armoury made Rifles, breeches punch. 16 v 18 Section D.A.C. annual umble f breeches.	

W.L.M. Laughlin Major A.V.C
O.A.D.V.S. 85 Div

WAR DIARY
INTELLIGENCE SUMMARY
(Erase heading not required.)

Army Form C. 2118

Place	Date	Hour	Summary of Events and Information	Remarks and references to Appendices
N-CAMP. KITCHENER'S CORNER.	1/11/17		[illegible handwritten entries]	
"	2/11/17			
"	3/11/17			
"	4/11/17			

WAR DIARY or INTELLIGENCE SUMMARY

Army Form C. 2118

Place	Date	Hour	Summary of Events and Information	Remarks and references to Appendices
J CAMP	3/11/17		Inspected 159 H.A. Bde. 4 x 13 Batteries condition good. C & D " " (Plenty guns but some unsuited in the Right sides the guns & condition very muddy.) Inspected 159 H.Q. Bde. Rooms changed to night condition. E. Battery Zone 180 Charge mature equip. Reed some & elevation - Demolition in need traction to Battle trajectories. Work much tenth to to form thrown. Reverted to PROVEN in charge of D.A.P. Conference of XIX Corps Hd 26.	
PROVEN	4/11/17		Inspected following units:— 105 Hty. Sdt. 2 km detained in port condition. Roles at under cover. " 16 Ukrainies limited spares obtained in the open. " 15 " Condition spares found. Ammn under cover. " 1. Re-mounted (one Aust Mounp) " 1.07 Australian. Removed in the open. Condition may prove.	

WAR DIARY or INTELLIGENCE SUMMARY

Army Form C. 2118

Place	Date	Hour	Summary of Events and Information	Remarks and references to Appendices
PROVEN	8.11.17		P/A Lieut. Smith & L.W.A.V.C. reported to 106' Fld. Amb. for duty in charge of Transport personnel, animals.	
"	9.11.17		Reported the following units:— 14' Gloucesters Cavalry; Coach parts; Animals in the approx. 15' Wo. Northn. Derby; Animals in poor condition; not their type. I.P.R. for innoculation. 105' M.T.Co.; Condition good. Places to linier very bad. No 3. Co. 10.T.C.; Condition very poor. Animals in the open. 106' Fd. Ambulance. Condition very poor. " " "	
"	9.11.17		Reported the following units:— 106' Fd. R.E.; 17' Pompol duts; 19' D.T.E.; 10' N.T.E.; 17' float pals; 106' M.T.C. All moved in the open with exception of a few animals, which mostly. Condition fairly good. Troops never under Strength, against the whom attempt being made to 3 new horse orders of 106' F. Amb. 45 M.V.S. new location at PROVEN.	
"	10.11.17		Reported the following units:— 204' P.C.; R.E. & 205' Y. & R.E. Condition: general good. Linier very muddy. " 241' M.T.C. Condition poor. Horseshoes P.L.B. Wade for unloading. " 106' G. M.T.C. Condition very poor. Linier in open or annex.	

Army Form C. 2118

WAR DIARY
or
INTELLIGENCE SUMMARY
(Erase heading not required.)

Instructions regarding War Diaries and Intelligence Summaries are contained in F. S. Regs., Part II. and the Staff Manual respectively. Title Pages will be prepared in manuscript.

Place	Date	Hour	Summary of Events and Information	Remarks and references to Appendices
PROVEN	11.11.17		Inspected 104' Field Amb HQ & B.; Condition rather sketchy; M.I.Z.; O.Rs.; + 20" Z.P.; + 23" Manchester Regt. Condition passed good. " 104' M.I.R.; Condition good. " N.2 C. A.T.C. " " " All arrivals on above standing without covers, with exception of 17.Z.P., without a standing. " 105' F. Ambulance; Condition very good; Baird standing without cover.	
"	12.11.17		4.5" M.M.P. evacuated sick at Admissions Centre. Inspected MMQ at PROVEN.	
"	13.11.17		Inspected 106' F. Ambulance. Condition very good; Standing in open. " 3 S' Dressed " Condition good; Under shelter.	
"	14.11.17		Attended Conference at XIV Corps A.Q.	
"	15.11.17		Arranged with A.D.V.S. 2nd Corps for the 4.5" M.M.P. to return over from 50' Div.	

Army Form C. 2118

WAR DIARY
or
INTELLIGENCE SUMMARY
(Erase heading not required.)

Instructions regarding War Diaries and Intelligence Summaries are contained in F. S. Regs., Part II. and the Staff Manual respectively. Title Pages will be prepared in manuscript.

Place	Date	Hour	Summary of Events and Information	Remarks and references to Appendices
PROVEN	16.11.17.		Interviewed D.A.D.V.S. 5th Divn. at Border Camp.	
BORDER CAMP.	17.11.17.		Proceeded to BORDER CAMP with D.H.Q. Inspected 45 MV1 at A.20.d.9.4.	
"	18.11.17.		Inspected A & D Batteries 159 Bde. D. Battery condition yourself good. Most in the open. One shelter for some mules (treatment). A. Battery. Condition poor. 22 Mules under cover. Sick cases under cover.	
"	19.11.17.		Inspected 35 D.A.C. No. 1. Section; Condition good; 50% mules under cover. No. 2 " " 60 % " " No. 3 " " No cover. " " Veterinary duties continuing arrangements.	
"	20.11.17.		Inspected No. 1. C. A.T.C.; Condition excellent; On hard standing in open. " C. 136, 159 Bde.; Condition yourself good; Under cover. " B " " " " any good; 25 % under cover; other in standings.	

WAR DIARY
or
INTELLIGENCE SUMMARY
(Erase heading not required.)

Place	Date	Hour	Summary of Events and Information	Remarks and references to Appendices
BORDER CAMP.	21.11.17		Inspected 106' Infy Bde. All animals under shelter with exception of some Mules belonging to N.Z.F.C. Condition of animals generally good. No horse standings at Water troughs, or surroundings deep in mud. " 106' M.G.Co.: Condition: good : Under shelter. " 104' M.G.Co. : Condition very good.	
"	22.11.17		Inspected Bat. 2'n 106' Infy Bde. " 16' Cheshire + 15' Nfp. Pleasant Trenches. Condition generally good : Trenchmork under water.	
"	23.11.17		Inspected 104' Infy Bde. " 17 " " " Under cover : Condition generally good. " 18 " " " " " " " " 20 " " " Under cover : " " " 23" Manchesters: Under cover: Some men in open; Condition generally good. " 15' Cheshires : Under cover. Condition generally good. Accommodation 1: R. " 14' Loyal N. Lancs " " " " " " 1: R + 1. L. D. " 241" M.G.Co. " & others open. Condition good. 1: R. form truck.	
"	24.11.17		Attended conference of Div'l D.D.V.T. at II'nd Corps Advanced H.Q.	

WAR DIARY
or
INTELLIGENCE SUMMARY.

Army Form C. 2118.

Place	Date	Hour	Summary of Events and Information	Remarks and references to Appendices
BORDER CAMP.	25/11/17		Inspected 157" F.A. Bde. A. Bty Condition poor. B " " poor. C " " poor. D " " poor. Yet made. Shelter for 75% of command, but no floors. Shelter for 75% of ammunition in each battery.	
"	26/11/17		Inspected them to 38' D.A.C. inspected with chain stencils. Guns not up to to be in a cave of concrete. 27 Line N.O. horses attached 14.9.11.Bde. Condition of these seem very poor. Coats rough & dirty. Feet anyway attention.	
"	27/11/17		Inspected 105" 106" 107" Fd Ambulances. 106' wounds under cover. Huts of 105 & 107 in open. Condition poor. Capt. R.H. STALKER, A.V.C. reports for duty from No.2. V.N in relief to Capt. F.F. HORTON.A.V.C.	
"	28/11/17		Inspected entraining of sick horses at PESELHOEK. Inspected 203", 204 & 205" F.C. R.E. All animals under shelter. Condition generally good.	

Army Form C. 2118.

WAR DIARY
or
INTELLIGENCE SUMMARY.
(Erase heading not required.)

Instructions regarding War Diaries and Intelligence Summaries are contained in F. S. Regs., Part II. and the Staff Manual respectively. Title pages will be prepared in manuscript.

Place	Date	Hour	Summary of Events and Information	Remarks and references to Appendices
BEROIER CAMP	29.11.17		Infantry & horses of C/159 F.A. Bde. inspected with their drivers. Examined. I have that officers slightly affected with lymphatic mumps:- Capt. F.P. Horton M.V.C. proceeded to No. 13 V.H. for duty.	
"	30.11.17		Infantry & horses of A/159 F.A. & 12bde inspected with their drivers. Own do not noticeable amount. 2nd Line transport to 5th, 23, 34, 48, 106, M.F.A. Bdes. Condition generally good, but numerous minor casualties among the animals.	

W.H. Taylor, Major, A.V.C.
D.A.D.V.S. 35th Div

Army Form C. 2118.

WAR DIARY of D.A.D.V.S. 35th Div. 1.12.17 to 31.12.17. Volume 12.

or

INTELLIGENCE SUMMARY.

(Erase heading not required.)

Instructions regarding War Diaries and Intelligence Summaries are contained in F. S. Regs., Part II. and the Staff Manual respectively. Title pages will be prepared in manuscript.

Vol 23

Place	Date	Hour	Summary of Events and Information	Remarks and references to Appendices
BORDER CAMP	1.12.17		Inspected sick horses at 45th M.V.I. for evacuation to horse home to Argued La. Condition generally good.	
"	2.12.17		Met remount train at PROVEN & inspected all remounts from 35th Div. Arrived in four ventilation, made good.	
"	3.12.17		Inspected entraining of sick horses at PESELHOEK for 2 XIV Corps. Noises front during the night late arrivals.	
"	4.12.17		Inspected the following Units at SIEGE-CAMP. 2.3rd Ambulation : Under cover with exception of a few mules. Condition generally good. " 20. 7. S. : Under cover. Condition generally good. " 19. 7. S. : Under cover with exception of a few mules. Condition generally good. " 10. 7. S. : Under cover ; Plan of ventilation wants correction. " 105th M. 7 Co : Stable shelter with exception of some mules. Condition good. Report returns copy to D.D.V.S. " 105th Rd. Mt 2Co : and huge which is being erected to be numbered. No 6 not in use. Under cover ; Wantage to having among the mules. Near the foundry but without stable mounts.	
"	5.12.17		Inspected Ho. & s14, Mr A.V.C. Veterinary equipment. Condition good. Under cover. Clean & complete.	

Army Form C. 2118.

WAR DIARY
or
INTELLIGENCE SUMMARY.
(Erase heading not required.)

Instructions regarding War Diaries and Intelligence Summaries are contained in F. S. Regs., Part II. and the Staff Manual respectively. Title pages will be prepared in manuscript.

Place	Date	Hour	Summary of Events and Information	Remarks and references to Appendices
BORDER CAMP.	6.12.17		Infants 19th Bn. Northumberland Fusiliers. Inoculation parade. Whole Battalion. No inoculation. No.1 & A.I.C. In open on hard standing. Inoculation to anoculation parade.	
"	7.12.17		Infants 35 August Co. Inoculation wing parade. Attendance in open on parade ground. Sick at H.5 M.V.1. for examination to hospital.	
"	8.12.17		Infants N. 1. Co. Div Train. Attended in open on hard standing. Inoculation wing parade. 10th Bn. N.Z.L.I. Inoculation made since Inoculation general parade. Several men with one cont to M.I.R. 19 " B.R.A. " " " parade.	
"	9.12.17		Inspected sick parade at M.V.1. for examination to hospital.	
"	10.12.17		Inspected H.5 M.V.1. to move to HAMHOEK on the 11th inst.	
COUTHOVE CHATEAU.	11.12.17		Moved to COUTHOVE - CHATEAU with D.H.Q. H.5 M.V.1. moved to HAMHOEK.	

WAR DIARY
INTELLIGENCE SUMMARY.

Army Form C. 2118.

Place	Date	Hour	Summary of Events and Information	Remarks and references to Appendices
COUTHOVE CHATEAU	12.12.17		Inspected 45" M.V.S. at HAMHOEK.	
"	13.12.17		Inspected 106" F. Amb. at PROVEN. Unremounts made afebrile. Condition very good. Veterinary equipment complete & clean. Capt. C.Y. Thompson A.V.C. promoted to temp. Lieut. to return to England.	
"	14.12.17		Visited the stabling arrangements of ARNEKE; M.T. V.P. Sp 137 & 139; Hdqrs R.Y.A.; & instructed them to evacuate sick men to St. OMER.	
"	15.12.17		Attended conference of D.A.D.V.S. at 2nd Corps H.Q. Hospital at 2.45 M? 9. 6. Unremounts under cover. Condition good.	
"	16.12.17		Inspected the following units :- 15" Squadron; Remounts 1 male ant specific ophthalmia. & 1 Mule for debility, very old. 14" Squadron; Remounts 1. R. Thermic Lameness. 16" " & 10 S' Pdn N.Q. 105" M.T.C.; Remounts 1. L.B. Mule very old & weak. 204" F.C.R.E. " 1. L.D. sole fistula near sesamoids. 35" Tunnel. Co. " All animals under shelter & condition generally good. Watering tents from streams where surroundings very muddy.	

Army Form C. 2118.

WAR DIARY
or
INTELLIGENCE SUMMARY.
(Erase heading not required.)

Instructions regarding War Diaries and Intelligence Summaries are contained in F. S. Regs., Part II. and the Staff Manual respectively. Title pages will be prepared in manuscript.

Place	Date	Hour	Summary of Events and Information	Remarks and references to Appendices
OOSTHOVE CHATEAU	17.12.17		Reports the following units:— 106 Fld. N.J. Twin anstastyl H. Mor N. Stafford Condition generally good. 19. D. Z. L. Guts 2 N.J. relieving inspection of armp; remarks to N.M.T. 14. Royal Scots Condition generally good. 18 N.T.	
"	18.12.17		Reports 203" F. by R.E. Condition generally good.	
"	19.12.17		Reports 45 M.V.T. in marching order. Equipment down & complete. 106 M. f. b. booklin & ammunit. generally good.	
"	20.12.17		Reports 5 Rounds from CHAIS & Installation inspection to units. 19' D. Z. f. & detaches on park corner & steam cleaning. 106 M. f. b. boiler anti-freezing	
"	21.12.17		Reports the following units:— M. 8. G. A. C. 10 hr Fld. Auk 26, 10X 20, 2 Y6 ; 23rd Manchester ; 10 H [crossed out] M. f. b. 105 + 109 f. Ambulance; Vet: equipment in good condition. Condition of animal motor factory; fair from with inspection of Lorries, & MS & G.S.T.C.	

Army Form C. 2118.

WAR DIARY
or
INTELLIGENCE SUMMARY.
(Erase heading not required.)

Instructions regarding War Diaries and Intelligence Summaries are contained in F. S. Regs., Part II. and the Staff Manual respectively. Title pages will be prepared in manuscript.

Place	Date	Hour	Summary of Events and Information	Remarks and references to Appendices
COUTHOVE	22.12.17		Conducted ride at N.I.T. for ammunition to limber. (Ramie bred for horse transport (hard front).)	
"	23.12.17		Conducted 203rd F.C. RE. Condition present good. 1 Remount with Ringworm. " 105th M.G. Co. Three mites conducted measures. Does not appear to be mange.	
"	24.12.17		Conducted 25th Rupind Co. Condition present good.	
"	25.12.17		Considerable full to remount. Remise here for horse transports.	
"	26.12.17		Remise for shipping & book for animal transports. Shipper full of snow.	
"	27.12.17		Conducted transport to following units:— 106 Inf. Bgd. & M. F.C. Condition generally good. 10th F.G. R.E. of 241st M.F.C. Condition apparent. Horses in ther condition.	

WAR DIARY
or
INTELLIGENCE SUMMARY.

(Erase heading not required.)

Army Form C. 2118.

Place	Date	Hour	Summary of Events and Information	Remarks and references to Appendices
COUTHOVE	28.12.17		Inspected 105 hy. Bde & M.T. Co. Sanitation found good. All under shelter. 205 T.C. R.E. Under canvas. Sanitation good. Rennch latrines. Rear front. Rough stationary.	
"	29.12.17		Inspected No. 39 L.C. A.T.C. Landed 6 Lower fevers; convulsive fever.	
"	30.12.17		Inspected 19th & 4th F.B. Examination 1. R for ophthalmia & I.W.D. for debility. Sprained condition of animals good; few horses hippic. Manse & shelter in bad condition. Peripneumonia brighter; purchase straw; awaiting letter for disinfection.	
"	31.12.17		Inspected horse with skin disease in No.11 Section D.A.C. Probably sarcoptic mange. D. Battery 159th F.A.Bde. Condition good & proper. Rounds aeroplane hand-fort amounts.	

W.N. Pughe, Major. A.V.C.
Q.A.D.V.S. 35 Div.

WAR DIARY of D.A.D.V.S. 35th Div.

INTELLIGENCE SUMMARY

Army Form C. 2118.

D.A.D.V.S., 35TH DIVISION.
No. 28/1
Date 2/2/18

1.1.18 to 31.1.18
Vol. I.

Place	Date	Hour	Summary of Events and Information	Remarks and references to Appendices
COUTHOVE	1.1.18		Inspected 261st M.T.C. Condition of animals good. 35 Inspected L.s Ambulance horses. Nearly front countries.	
"	2.1.18		Inspected nuts of 106th Fld Amb & M.T.C. transactions normal & treatment under functions them commenced.	
"	3.1.18		Inspected 205 Fd Co. R.E. on to driving in. Having an whole good; one just them fut. Condition of animals generally good.	
"	4.1.18		Inspected detachment of 63 animals from 35 D.A.C. Condition good. Condition fair. 35 Trench Mortar Battery horses for transport. New front continues.	
"	5.1.18		Handed over to O.C. A.S. M.V.T. Proceeded on 14 days leave to ENGLAND.	

Army Form C. 2118.

WAR DIARY
or
INTELLIGENCE SUMMARY.
(Erase heading not required.)

Instructions regarding War Diaries and Intelligence Summaries are contained in F. S. Regs., Part II. and the Staff Manual respectively. Title pages will be prepared in manuscript.

Place	Date	Hour	Summary of Events and Information	Remarks and references to Appendices
COUTHOVE	6.1.18		Inspects all units at M.V.1. for innoculation to Prophylate.	
"	7.1.18		Interviewed units drawn for the Bven at PESELHOEK.	
"	8.1.18		Inspected drawn of 15" Imperial Div. Ambulances audio features.	
"	9.1.18		Moved to WELSH FARM on change to D.M.O.	
WELSH FARM	10.1.18		Inspected drawn of 5" Traffic Control argumentum. Ambulance fun.	
"	11.1.18		" " 17" N.Z. T. Ambulance fund.	
"	12.1.18		" Anumals 2nd "M.T. Co Ambulance any fuma	
"	13.1.18		Inspected units for innoculation to Prophylate.	
"	14.1.18		Interviewed units drawn for Prophylate.	
"	15.1.18		Examined manpower from a unu of Pack Mhmps from A.154 F.A. Rules with respective units.	
"	16.1.18		Inspected drawn to M.V.I. G. A.T.C.	
"	17.1.18		Inspected units drawn for innoculation to Prophylate.	
"	18.1.18		Inspected monument from CALAIS before noon.	
"	19.1.18		Distributed amounts to Unit, with the D.A.P.M.S.	

WAR DIARY
or
INTELLIGENCE SUMMARY.
(Erase heading not required.)

Army Form C. 2118.

Place	Date	Hour	Summary of Events and Information	Remarks and references to Appendices
WALSH FARM	20.1.18		Took over from O.C. 45" M.V.T, on return from leave.	
"	21.1.18		Reports arms ammo to A/159 F.A. Bde. Dungannon "Rio".	
			" equipment to 45 M.V.T to sent to December Wksp & found it wants.	
			" 45 M.V.T & with ammunition for ammunition.	
"	22.1.18		Reports 159 F.A. Bde.	
			A. Bty.; Condition very good.	
			B " " "	
			C " good.	
			D " generally poor, not as big as other batteries.	
			Hmm. 3 distant sun shells & magazine been mutual.	
"	23.1.18		Reports A Bty 159" F.A. Bde. Ammunition very good. Few casualties.	
			" C " " " "	
			All made good.	
"	24.1.18		Reports B. Bty. 157" F.A. Bde. Ammunition generally good. Whole ammo.	
			" D " " " " Condition good. No ammo.	
			" 18h. 26, 106" Bty. Bde. Condition good.	
			" 15" Phoenix. Ammunition good. Ammunition date, 1. P.R. for luminous.	
			" 105" M.F.G. " "	

Army Form C. 2118.

WAR DIARY
or
INTELLIGENCE SUMMARY.
(Erase heading not required.)

Instructions regarding War Diaries and Intelligence Summaries are contained in F. S. Regs., Part II. and the Staff Manual respectively. Title pages will be prepared in manuscript.

Place	Date	Hour	Summary of Events and Information	Remarks and references to Appendices
WELSH FARM.	25.1.18		Inspected 105 F. Ambulance. Condition good. " 106 F. Ambulance. Condition good. " 107 F. Ambulance. Condition good. Own cases of lice among the wounded.	
"	26.1.18		Inspected 203rd F.C. R.E. " 204th " " 19 St Sanitary. 14 Laboratory. All under cover & condition very good. Free from other diseases & few casualties.	
"	27.1.18		Inspected 105 Bde Fld Amb. 15 " " Workshops 16 " " Condition of animals good. All under cover. Few casualties. " Nos 2, 3 & 4 Coys. A.S.C. Condition excellent. Free from serious f.a.k.	
"	28.1.18		Inspected 17 Royal Fus. 4 M. & G.B 19 D.I.L. F.i. 241st M.G.C. Condition personnel good. M. I Coys horses in poor form & few casualties. 106 M.G. Cos.	

Army Form C. 2118.

WAR DIARY
or
INTELLIGENCE SUMMARY.
(Erase heading not required.)

Instructions regarding War Diaries and Intelligence Summaries are contained in F. S. Regs., Part II. and the Staff Manual respectively. Title pages will be prepared in manuscript.

Place	Date	Hour	Summary of Events and Information	Remarks and references to Appendices
CANAL BANK.	29.1.18		Moved to CANAL BANK. Inspected No.1. Section 35" D.A.C. Condition of horses excellent. Mules poor. " No. 2. Section " Condition of horses excellent. Mules poor. " No. 3. Section " Condition of Mules poor.	
"	30.1.18		Inspected 104" Bde. Nd. 2tn. Condition very poor. " 23rd Manufactus Condition: Horses " 104" M.g.C. " very poor.	
"	31.1.18		Inspected M.T.g. " Condition very poor. Remounts 1 V.O. for mules & not up to its march. " 18"L.Y. " Condition poor. " 20"L.Y. Condition poor.	

1.2.18

W. N. Y---- Major A.V.C.
O.d. D.V.1 35" Div

Army Form C. 2118.

WAR DIARY of D.A.D.V.S. 35th Div.

INTELLIGENCE SUMMARY 1.2.18 to 28.2.18 Vol. II

(Erase heading not required.)

D.A.D.V.S.,
35TH DIVISION.
No. 3.2.S
Date 1/3/18

Place	Date	Hour	Summary of Events and Information	Remarks and references to Appendices
CANAL BANK C.25.c.7.5 Sheet 2B	1.2.18		Inspected detachments of No.3. Section at KEMPTON PARK Condition good.	
"			" 10th Hy. Bde at " " Neither on wintering. Manure not removed.	
"	2.2.18		Attended a conference at II Corps Head Qrs. Inspected 2.0.5.? L.b.R.E. Condition emp good. Veterinary equipment satisfactory.	
			" C.R.E's horses. Condition good.	
"	3.2.18		Inspected No.1. 6. 35 Div. Train. Attached 2nd line horses of 23rd A.F.A. Bde. Condition of animals generally good.	
"	4.2.18		Inspected Veterinary Equipment of 157th F.A. Bde. 3 Unit charts required, otherwise satisfactory.	
"	5.2.18		Inspected 12. N.F.P. Condition emp good.	
			" Veterinary Equipment of 159th F.A. Bde. Condition of equipment emp good.	
"	6.2.18		Inspected Veterinary equipment of 45th M.V.T. Condition satisfactory.	
			" sick animals for evacuation to base hospital.	

WAR DIARY
or
INTELLIGENCE SUMMARY.
(Erase heading not required.)

Army Form C. 2118.

Place	Date	Hour	Summary of Events and Information	Remarks and references to Appendices
CANAL BANK	7.2.18		Reports Veterinary Equipment & sick arrival in following units :— 14" Gloucester, 19" N. Fusiliers, 203" F.C. R.E., 204" " ", 205" " ". Four casualties. Equipment satisfactory.	
ELVERDINGHE	8.2.18		Moved with 13 Echelon to ELVERDINGHE CHATEAU. Reports with arrival at 45" M.V.S.	
"	9.2.18		Attended conference at D.M.S. H.Q. Evacuated 28" Manchesters. 1 fract. skull.	
"	10.2.18		Inspected 49" Remount Mules arrival to 35" D.V.C from No. 5 Res. Remount Depot CALAIS. Evacuated 1 for Purulent Ophthalmia, 1 for tumour on neck to 1 fract. Mange. Report sent to other units occupied ⅌ 203, 204 & 205 ♀ G.R.E. & veterinarians them to 2" Corp. to ascertain to all parts to which the horses are attached.	
"	11.2.18		Reports 107" F. Ambulance. Conditions, pairment, groom. Cases sent evacuation for Suf. Mange. M.M.P. pains & C.R.A's horses. Condition, ration, satisfactory.	

Army Form C. 2118.

WAR DIARY
or
INTELLIGENCE SUMMARY.
(Erase heading not required.)

Place	Date	Hour	Summary of Events and Information	Remarks and references to Appendices
ELVERDINGHE	12.2.18		Inspected sick animals at H.S. M.V.S. Veterinary equipment & sick animals to following units:- 10" N.I.F. Equipment complete. Condition of animals generally good. " " " " " " " " " 19.D.I. " " " " " "	
"	13.2.18		Inspected Veterinary Equipment & sick of the following units. 241st M.G.C. " " " " " " 106" M.G.C. Animals in general good condition. Equipment satisfactory.	
"	14.2.18		Inspected 10 5" F. Ambulance Condition of animals good. Vet. equipment complete & satisfactory. Verify uniform to V.G.I.	
"	15.2.18		Inspected the following units:- 15" Divisional 104" M.G.C. Condition of animals general good. Immaterial I.N.D. for Divisional Schools Wkshp. Base on F.C. Mkg 157 F.A. Bde & minor incidents no vaccines to hand with regard to lightning for lightning.	
"	16.2.18		Inspected the following units:- A"Bty 157 F.A. Bde. General cases of lice. Grooming unsatisfactory. Condition generally good. C" " " " " " " " " " Grooming general. Hand ferrets. Veterinary equipment satisfactory.	

WAR DIARY
or
INTELLIGENCE SUMMARY

Army Form C. 2118.

Place	Date	Hour	Summary of Events and Information	Remarks and references to Appendices
ELVERDINGHE	17.2.18		Inspected the following Units:— B. Bty. 167" A.A. Bde. Ammunition, personnel, horses & guns shown in light condition	
"			" D. Bty. Ammunition, personnel, horses: a few in light condition as recommended range for them.	
"	18.2.18		Inspected 106" M.T.C. Ammunition of arms good. Veterinary equipment complete.	
"			" 17" T.S.C. Ammunition of horses & mules satisfactory.	
"	19.2.18		Inspected 159" F.A. Bde. A. Bty.: Ammunition very good. B. " : excellent. C. " : fair to good. Harnessing arms. Some cases of lice. D. " : good. Horse poorly informed.	
			Report sent to C.C.	
"	20.2.18		Inspected 4.5" M.V.V.T. Gun precautions taken & found it active frostbite. 55" Signal Co. Harness in good condition.	
"	21.2.18		Inspected 4" W.H.H./6.4pm. Condition again. Went onforward of V.G.	

Army Form C. 2118.

Instructions regarding War Diaries and Intelligence Summaries are contained in F. S. Regs., Part II. and the Staff Manual respectively. Title pages will be prepared in manuscript.

WAR DIARY
or
INTELLIGENCE SUMMARY.
(Erase heading not required.)

Place	Date	Hour	Summary of Events and Information	Remarks and references to Appendices
ELVERDINGHE.	22.2.18		Inspected units remains at H.S. M.V.T. for evacuation to Base Hospital.	
"	23.2.18		Inspected the following units:- 20 3" S.G. R.E. 20 A " " 20 5 " " Institute personnel parade "Evacuates 1 O.R. O from 203 L.A.E. for inventory	
"	24.2.18		Attended Conference at 2" Corps "Rome Quarters.	
"	25.2.18		Inspected 19 Mjr. D.T.T. Condition present good. Three N.O. isolated for eruption on legs; 20 Remount Coy. recruits + found them apparently free from disease. Visit at H.S. M.V.T.	
"	26.2.18		Inspected 106 F. Ambulance at ROUSBRUGGE. Visited to ascertain many forms.	
"	27.2.18		Inspected unit horses of 157 F.A.B. Plea. Casualties normal in number. Inoculated anti-typhoid. A horse belonging to 19 D.T.C. under observation for skin disease, nettles on 25 Welt. Pompon anti-pustery.	

Army Form C. 2118.

WAR DIARY
or
INTELLIGENCE SUMMARY.
(Erase heading not required.)

Place	Date	Hour	Summary of Events and Information	Remarks and references to Appendices
EVERDINGHE	20.2.18		Infantile 30 remount mules arrived to 35th D.A.C. Evacuated one unsound mule to remounts. 6 mules remount to D.A.C. Few casualties & treatment only (practising injections) this month. Lines of trenches everywhere inspected from 6 different units.	

W.H. Taylor Lt
R.A.V.C.
D.A.D.V.S. / 35th Div.

Army Form C. 2118.

WAR DIARY of A.D.V.S. 35th Div. Vol. III

INTELLIGENCE SUMMARY. from 1.3.18 to 31.3.18

(Erase heading not required.)

D.A.D.V.S.
35TH DIVISION.
No. 504
Date 1/4/18

Place	Date	Hour	Summary of Events and Information	Remarks and references to Appendices
ELVERDINGHE	1.3.18		Infantry. Horse reported with other shivers in C/159 Bde R.F.A. Animal appears to be affected with mange & to be evacuated to M.V.I. Instructions given than evacuation necessary to be without infantry extra ration to C. Battery but failed to detect any further cases. Infantry sick animal at M.V.I. for evacuation to home. Heart front.	
"	2.3.18		Infantry sick animals in 159 F.A. Bde., & 35 D.A.C. Casualties normal. Important actic function. Evacuated 1 Remount Mule suspected of mange. Front & mane - cold winds.	
"	3.3.18		Infantry. 10 5" Vide Transport animals. 15" Pyorrhoea - condition poor. 15 Chilairia condition good. Not in pool in Shaments. 4 N. Italy; condition fairly good. Some horses not in good condition. A number of these have been recently clipped.	
"	4.3.18		Infantry. 203, 204, & 205 F.A.i.s sick animals. Evacuated 1 to 1.8 from 204 & 41 R. Corps 2.13.6. both name cases. Casualties fewer & treatments audio function. " sick animal at 45 M.V.I.	

Army Form C. 2118.

D.A.D.V.S.
35TH DIVISION.
No. 504
Date. 14/3/18

WAR DIARY
or
INTELLIGENCE SUMMARY.
(Erase heading not required.)

Instructions regarding War Diaries and Intelligence Summaries are contained in F. S. Regs., Part II. and the Staff Manual respectively. Title pages will be prepared in manuscript.

Place	Date	Hour	Summary of Events and Information	Remarks and references to Appendices
ELVERDINGHE	5.3.18		Inspected 10 & 13th (Infantry) transports arrived. 12" N.Z.I.; Condition of horses & gearing very good. 15" N.Z.I.; Horses poor. Mules generally poor, but not as good as the horses. 19" Royal Scots; Horses in poor condition; Mules poorly poor. Stock animals in fair condition.	
"	6.3.18		Inspected A.12th, 159" F.A. Bde. Condition poor. Found cases of lice. Present nutrition to be stopped out with onions & 35" O.A.S. Four unmounted Mules with Chronic Infections of Pasterns & previously have evacuated to hospital.	
"	7.3.18		Inspected rest of 159" F.A. Bde. Cumulative form & treatment inclination. " C. Bty " " " Condition. Personnel found becoming not good. Issued orders to this events to ambulation issued for clothing & dressings. Weekly conferences to V.Os.	

Army Form C. 2118.

WAR DIARY
or
INTELLIGENCE SUMMARY.
(Erase heading not required.)

D.A.D.V.S.
35TH DIVISION.

No. 504
Date. 1/4/18

Instructions regarding War Diaries and Intelligence Summaries are contained in F. S. Regs., Part II. and the Staff Manual respectively. Title pages will be prepared in manuscript.

Place	Date	Hour	Summary of Events and Information	Remarks and references to Appendices
ELVERDINGHE	8.3.18		Inspected M.T.Y. 16. T.Y. 19. D.T.T. Units. Himself satisfactory. Arrival animals affects with trim on 19. T.Y. T.Y. & 19. D.T.T.	
"	9.3.18		Attended a conference at Adv. 2 Ech. 2nd Corps. Infantry with arrival on D.H.Q. Few casualties. Instant satisfactory. Divisional summary commences at 11 A.M.	
"	10.3.18		Inspected units of 159 F.A. Bde. Instant satisfactory. Few casualties. 19 D.T.T. " " 10 S. T. Ambulance. Condition good. Animal affects with trim.	
ST. SIXTE	11.3.18		Moved to ST. SIXTE in charge of D.H.Q. Inspected units arrivals for convenience at 115 M.V.T.	
"	12.3.18		Inspected units arrived with 55 Div. M. of Bde. En route I.R. to M.V.T. 19 Panjal Units & 10 N.T.T. with animals. Horses out of sight & markings satisfactory. Progress.	

Army Form C. 2118.

WAR DIARY
or
INTELLIGENCE SUMMARY.
(Erase heading not required.)

Instructions regarding War Diaries and Intelligence Summaries are contained in F. S. Regs., Part II. and the Staff Manual respectively. Title pages will be prepared in manuscript.

D.A.D.V.S.
35TH DIVISION.
No. 524
Date 1/4/18

Place	Date	Hour	Summary of Events and Information	Remarks and references to Appendices
ST. SIXTE	13.3.18		Inspected units of the following units :— 105° F.Amb.; No.1, 2, 3, Section D.A.C. Casualties nil in number to Veterinary veterinary Inspected animals in convoy to the "Dorrs chac Phylo" up w. vet. D.A.C. Horses appeared to improve on favour in its three mobility.	
"	14.3.18		Inspected units at 45 M.V.T. for evacuation. 19 Horses of 157° F.A.Bde. infected statique by shell fire, but evening sun argon line.	
"	15.3.18		Inspected units of 35°D.A.C. " " " of "Remonte" with Div.trem. All movements free from disease. Inspected sick animals with 19° M.V.D.Y.S. Two chair cases under observation. Progressing in its history.	
"	16.3.18		Inspected units of 157° F.A.Bde. Casualties normal + treatment under putting.	
"	17.3.18		Inspected 19° M.V.P. M.V.P. + evacuates L.h.O. Mule to Remo. Condition present poor. Consulted "N.L". Inspected units of 35°D.A.C.; Conditions under putting.	

Army Form C. 2118.

WAR DIARY
or
INTELLIGENCE SUMMARY.
(Erase heading not required.)

D.A.D.V.S.
35TH DIVISION
No .....504......
Date ...1/4/18....

Place	Date	Hour	Summary of Events and Information	Remarks and references to Appendices
ST. SIXTE	18.3.18		Inspected Nos. 2, 3 & 4 Coys. A.V.C. Condition very good. Few evacuations.	
"	19.3.18		Inspected 159' F.A. Bde. A. Bty: Condition good. A number of horses with lice. Instructions given to be clipped out & B " " " A few animals affected with lice to be clipped out " C " " " " " " " " " " " D " " " Practically free from lice.	
"	20.3.18.		Inspected 19' F.A. Bde. Condition good. Evacuated 1 strong mule & 1 Mule worn out. " 18 " " " " Evac'd 1 Mule for Mange (suspected) (V.G.) " 19 D.T.C. " " Evac'd 1 R. with chronic lameness.	
"	21.3.18		Attended a conference of A.D.V.Ss & D.A.D.V.Ss. Relief of D.V.1 at 2nd Army.	
"	22.3.18		A.D.V.1. 2nd Army Inspected the Horses of 159 F.A. 12 Bde.	
"	23.3.18	11.30 am	Entrained at PROVEN with D.H.Q. for HEILLY. Took charge of D.HQ. transport.	

Army Form C. 2118.

WAR DIARY
or
INTELLIGENCE SUMMARY.
(Erase heading not required.)

D.A.D.V.S.,
35TH DIVISION
No. 504.
Date 1/4/18

Instructions regarding War Diaries and Intelligence Summaries are contained in F.S. Regs., Part II. and the Staff Manual respectively. Title pages will be prepared in manuscript.

Place	Date	Hour	Summary of Events and Information	Remarks and references to Appendices
MARICOURT SUR SOMME	24.3.18		Took D.H.Q. transport from HEILLY to MERICOURT-SUR-SOMME. 7 A.M. Took D.H.Q. transport to BRAY-SUR-SOMME.	
BRAY-SUR-SOMME	25.3.18		Visited M.V.1 at MERCOURT. Inspected 205 & C.F.E. Condition of wounds satisfactory. Met A.D.V.S. 7 Corps at BRAY. 8 P.M. Moved to SAILLY LAURETTE with D.H.Q.	
HENENCOURT	26.3.18		Moved to HENENCOURT with D.H.Q. 45" M.V.1. moved to WARLOY.	
"	27.3.18		Inspected 105" & 106" Fys. Ptns. M. & Cars, 19" M.F.; 105" & 104" F. Ambulances. Condition of animals satisfactory. Met A.D.V.S. VII Corps at WARLOY.	
"	28.3.18.		Inspected 203" & 205" Co. R.I.F. Condition of animals good.	

Army Form C. 2118.

WAR DIARY
or
INTELLIGENCE SUMMARY.

(Erase heading not required.)

D.A.D.V.S.
35TH DIVISION.

No. ....
Date ....

Place	Date	Hour	Summary of Events and Information	Remarks and references to Appendices
HENENCOURT	29.3.18		Inspected 1 S.G. 4. F.A. Bde. Unable to ascend any front. Water some casualties from shell fire.	
"	30.3.18		Inspected 157 F.A. Bde. Condition very poor. Watering from pond, not from river. Numerous casualties from shell fire.	
PONT NOYELLES	31.3.18		Moved with D.H.Q. 15 PONT-NOYELLES & took charge of transport of 5th M.V.S. moved to CONTAY & heated with 151 G.A.S. on account of instructions received from VII Corps. Found instructions that an onward shuttle owning traffic in CONTAY- ST-GRATIEN-FRECHENCOURT on account of Divisional Footpaths. no orders from VII Corps.	

W. M. L. Taylor Major A.V.C.
D.A.D.V.S. 35th Div.

Army Form C. 2118.

WAR DIARY of D.A.D.V.S. 35-Div.
Vol. II 1.4.18 to 30.4.18

INTELLIGENCE SUMMARY

(Erase heading not required.)

Place	Date	Hour	Summary of Events and Information	Remarks and references to Appendices
PONT NOYELLES	1.4.18		Inspected with Farrier Serjt 45th M.V.S. at COOTAY. 45th M.V.S. moved to QUERRIEU.	
"	2.4.18		Inspected 104th Bty & 106th Bty Bdr. Condition to animals good. Ammunition animals 19th T.M.B. Condition of animals good.	
"	3.4.18		Inspected 104th T. Ambulance. Condition of animals very good. No casualties. No. 1 C.A.T.C. Condition to animals very poor. No casualties	
"	4.4.18		Inspected Remount for Artillery & Infy Bde. Condition poorly found & frame from shrinence.	
"	5.4.18		Inspected No. 1 C.A.T.C. Condition of animals rather frightening with for ammunition at 45th M.V.S.	
"	6.4.18		Moved with D.HQ to PUCHEVILLERS. 45th M.V.S. moved "	

Army Form C. 2118.

WAR DIARY
or
INTELLIGENCE SUMMARY.

(Erase heading not required.)

Instructions regarding War Diaries and Intelligence Summaries are contained in F. S. Regs., Part II. and the Staff Manual respectively. Title pages will be prepared in manuscript.

Place	Date	Hour	Summary of Events and Information	Remarks and references to Appendices
PUCHEVILLERS	7.4.18		Inspected 106th & 107th F. Ambulances. Condition of personnel satisfactory. Weather wet. Roads heavy for transport.	
"	8.4.18		Inspected animals of 105th Fd. Amb. Condition generally good. Roads heavy. Weather wet.	
TOUTENCOURT	9.4.18		Inspected 104 Fd. Amb. Condition of animals good. 203 " Co. R.E. } Condition of animal's good. 204 " " 205 " " Moved with O.M.G. to TOUTENCOURT. 15 M.V.T. moved to "	
"	10.4.18		Inspected Nos. 2, 3 & 4 Co. A.T.C. Condition of horses very good. Saw ammunition. Weather wet. Roads heavy.	
"	11.4.18		Met A.D.V.S. I Corps. Inspected 106 Infy. Bde. Condition of animals good. 1 " Mules of 19 Range Rifles in slight condition. L.S. M.G. Condition of animals very good. Weather conditions greatly improved.	

(A7092). Wt. W12839/M1293. 75,000. 1/17. D. D. & L., Ltd. Forms/C.2118/14.

WAR DIARY
or
INTELLIGENCE SUMMARY.

(Erase heading not required.)

Army Form C. 2118.

Place	Date	Hour	Summary of Events and Information	Remarks and references to Appendices
TOUTENCOURT	12.4.18		Inspected 35' Div. M.T.L. Condition of material satisfactory. B.L. deficient. 16 I.C. stators. " Inspected accounts of 4.5" M.V.I. to west of Mount C.O. & found it in order.	
"	13.4.18		Inspected 10.6" Howitzers. Little information. "Major Railton admitted to M.I.A from 20.6 R.E. affiliated with "Whatton Pin"; when I visited & between Church Monter. 4.5" M.V.I. surrendering its units to II bush anvrum Emmy station at BOULLENS as division 4-P 10 kilometres (on return left for D horses who returum to entrain after drawing them were to recovery Returning "Montrich". 157 & 159 P.A. Btres arrive now at FORCEVILLE. Apptymed to check pleasure at FORCEVILLE in bad state of repair. Interviewed the Major with the view to put it in ordermunk. met K.O.G. 157 & 159 Retn R.F.A.	
"	14.4.18		Inspected No. 3 Section D.A.C. Condition of material very poor. " visits to Ams 1 & 2. Return D.A.C. Ammunition figure & harritments satisfactory.	

Army Form C. 2118.

WAR DIARY
or
INTELLIGENCE SUMMARY.
(Erase heading not required.)

Place	Date	Hour	Summary of Events and Information	Remarks and references to Appendices
TOUTENCOURT	15.4.18		Inspected the following Units :— 15: Division : Condition of animals and equipment good. 15: Armoured A.M. Battery " " " " Ammunition Train " " " " 203rd, 204th, 205th Y. & L. R.E. Inspection of horses & mules poor. New ammunition Mule harness for horses in a bad state of repair & insufficient for number of animals.	
"	16.4.18		Inspected 104th Infy. Bde. 17, 7, Y.&L. Condition good. 18. " " " 19. D.L.I. " Ammunition: poor Inspected 105 & 107 F. Amb. Condition of animals very poor.	
"	17.4.18		Inspected 35th Div. M.G. Cr. Bn: Condition of animals & equipment good. Made arrangements for 3 officers with their horses and 3 Rickson apparatus and Maxim type. (Whither on Spartivento & Lewis.)	

Effects of Mustard Gas

Subject: Mustard Gas.   Copy Appendix A.

To A.D.V.S.
            5th Corps.

Ten cases of horses affected with "Mustard Gas" have been reported for the week ending April 18th 1918. It has been confined to Riders, and the cases occurred at SENLIS, which place has been heavily gas shelled.

It is likely that these animals have been ridden off the roads and across country in the vicinity of gas shell holes, thus becoming affected which would account for the cases being confined to Riders.

The skin has presented lesions similar to the effects of a severe cantharides blister, and varying in size from a few square inches to one or two square feet. The parts affected have been the delicate skin of the sheath, mammary glands, between the thighs, and inside the elbows. Patches have also been found about the pastern and heels.

The animals became very lame and incapacitated for several days, depending on the parts affected.

Cases are yielding to treatment with Whale Oil and Lead Acetate.

Instructions have been issued that Riders and other animals should not be taken in the vicinity of gas shell holes, if possible to avoid these.

D.H.Q.,
18/4/18.
                                    (Sd) W.H.Taylor, Major, A.V.C.
                                        D.A.D.V.S. 35th Div.

WAR DIARY or INTELLIGENCE SUMMARY

Army Form C. 2118.

(Erase heading not required.)

Place	Date	Hour	Summary of Events and Information	Remarks and references to Appendices
TOUTENCOURT	18.4.18		Worked conference of O.Cs. Affiliated to Munitions for an enemies machine. Copy of report on Mixture for urea as forwarded to A.D.V.S. 5 C.D. for month ending 18.4.18, attached and marked A.	A.
"	19.4.18		Evacuated 1/6 Rifle Bde. Condition good. 12 N.F. ? " " 18 N.F. ? " Besides too food condition. Made friar to gram. 19 Argyll Sctrs. Condition general good; lymphatic very poor. " 19 Northumberland Fusiliers. lymphatic very poor. Weather turned much colder. Snow + hail during the day.	
"	20.4.18		Evacuated 35 Div. train. No.1, 2, 3, 4 Cos. Condition of animals very poor. Emaciation fever. 1 animal destroyed 1 mangey bowls + 2 wounded. Equipment – shoes, musterings, incomplete.	
"	21.4.18		Evacuated B 1345 157 F.A. Bde. Condition good. " C " " " " " very good. " D " " " " " " Casualties: Fever + intestinal catarrh + rating. Shortage of shrapnel. D.W.B.O.T. returns to complete records.	

WAR DIARY
or
INTELLIGENCE SUMMARY.
(Erase heading not required.)

Army Form C. 2118.

Place	Date	Hour	Summary of Events and Information	Remarks and references to Appendices
TOUTENCOURT	22.4.18		Inspected animals at 106° F. Ambulance. Condition very good. Few casualties. Equipment complete.	
			Received 1.6.9 dust belonging to H.W. Phillips.	
			Course of depth thermopilation of water trains.	
"	23.4.18		Inspected 159° F.A. Bde. at VARENNES.	
			A. Bty. Condition very good.	
			B. " " " "	
			C. " " " "	
			D. " " good. Few casualties & health very good.	
"	24.4.18		Inspected No.1. Section 35° D.A.C. Condition of animals good.	
			" " 2 " " " " "	
			Casualties few; showing actin[?] footings.	
"	25.4.18		Water supply at HARPONVILLE quite inadequate; 1111 from one well.	
			Mules evacuated to Q. Branch.	
			Inspected 19° M.F. Condition very good.	

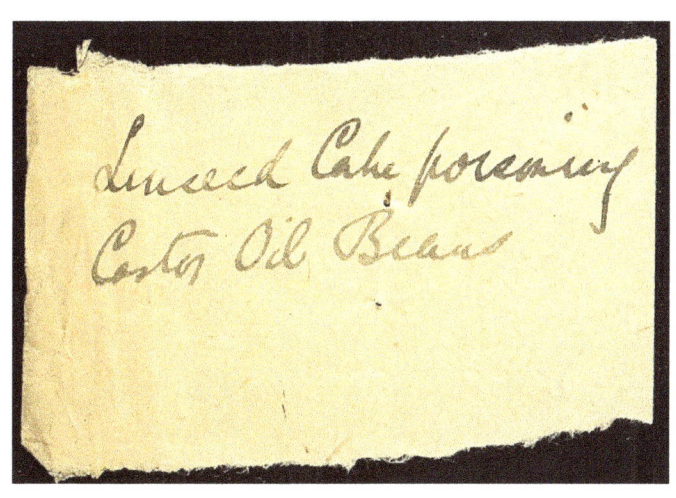

WAR DIARY
or
INTELLIGENCE SUMMARY.
(Erase heading not required.)

Army Form C. 2118.

Instructions regarding War Diaries and Intelligence Summaries are contained in F. S. Regs., Part II. and the Staff Manual respectively. Title pages will be prepared in manuscript.

Place	Date	Hour	Summary of Events and Information	Remarks and references to Appendices
TOUTENCOURT	26.4.18		Particulars A. Battery 157 F.A.Bde. Condition of ammunition. Casualties. Officers. Horses, anti-gas outfit. Veterinary equipment complete. Reports arts. at 4 S.M.V.I. Received wire from I.C. informing that issue of Linseed Cake has been stopped owing to source futures issues namely horses & that further will be discontinued. A.D.V.S. informed. He has also since been arrived to Division from some division.	
"	27.4.18		35' Div. Q. reports that 40ff of mules in being on increment at HARPONVILLE under attachment to 1st Bn. E.R.E. Visited the Board convened to that showing-smith of 6 C.C. Div. Train in accordance with S.R.O. 3668 No. 68 dated 12.3.18. Most of the men were not qualified to undertake shoes on [?] drawn on Issues 1210 K.R.	
"	28.4.18		Particulars of the following units:- 35' August; 17 I. F., 203, 204 & 20 S. Co. R.E. Casualties. Offrs. & Lieutenant. anti-gas outfit. Veterinary equipment complete.	

WAR DIARY
INTELLIGENCE SUMMARY
(Erase heading not required.)

Army Form C. 2118

Place	Date	Hour	Summary of Events and Information	Remarks and references to Appendices
TOUTENCOURT	29/4/18		Infants arrived & amounts with the following units:— 107th F. Amb.; 7th, 25, 106 Bde, 17 Royal Irish, 12 N.T.S., 18 M.T.C., 19 M.F.; 35 Signal Co. Casualties few in number & treatment under fracture.	
"	30/4/18		Infants arrived evacuation at Mobile Veterinary Section. Number of 106 F. Ambulance. Condition very good. Causalities few.	
			D.A.D. 1.5.18.	W.T. Taylor Major A.V.C. D.A.D.V.S. 35 Div.

Army Form C. 2118.

WAR DIARY of D.A.D.V.S. 35th Div.
Vol. V 1.5.18 to 31.5.18.
INTELLIGENCE SUMMARY
(Erase heading not required.)

D.A.D.V.S. 35TH DIVISION.
No. 753
Date 1/6/18

Instructions regarding War Diaries and Intelligence Summaries are contained in F. S. Regs., Part II. and the Staff Manual respectively. Title pages will be prepared in manuscript.

Place	Date	Hour	Summary of Events and Information	Remarks and references to Appendices
TOUTENCOURT	1.5.18		Inspected 35th M.G. Corps: A.C. Condition generally good.	
			B " " " "	
			C & D " " " Casualties few. Equipment complete.	
			Lines very crowded, owing to recent rain. Equipment complete.	
			All horse cover to be pushed in to stay.	
"	2.5.18		Infantry Brigade Transport moved to HÉRISSART & RUBEMPRÉ, which places are occupied by Brigade Trains (Military).	
			Visited these places with D.A.Q.M.G. to arrange for separate watering places for animals of Division.	
"	3.5.18		Inspected Remounts for issue to Div. Units:-	
			4.R: G.H.Q: 9 & 24 Mules. Rather of poor quality: N.O. fair: Mules on small side & condition only fair.	
			Division now in Reserve with exception of R.F.A.	

WAR DIARY
or
INTELLIGENCE SUMMARY.
(Erase heading not required.)

Army Form C. 2118.

Place	Date	Hour	Summary of Events and Information	Remarks and references to Appendices
TOUTENCOURT	4.5.18		Inspected 106th Infantry Bde:- 2nd. 2/6: Condition good. 17th Royal Scots: Condition generally good. A few mules in light condition. 12th N.F.: " " " 15th N.F.: " " "	
"	5.5.18		Inspected sick animals at M.V.T. for examination to leave Hospital	
HÉRISSART	6.5.18		Moved to HÉRISSART with D.M.O. Samples of water Lanisant sent to Base Hygiene Lab. BOULOGNE. for subject in fluid for horses (water not known manufacture.)	
"	7.5.18		Inspected 106th F. Ambulance & 19th Northumberland Fusiliers. Condition generally good. Few casualties.	
"	8.5.18		Inspected 104th Infantry Bde. 17th L.F.: Condition generally good. Few casualties. 18th " " " " " " 19th D.L.I. Condition poor. Amongst the animals two light horses more large measurements. Report sent to G.S. 19th D.L.I.	

WAR DIARY or INTELLIGENCE SUMMARY.

Army Form C. 2118.

(Erase heading not required.)

Place	Date	Hour	Summary of Events and Information	Remarks and references to Appendices
HERISSART	9.5.18		Reported the working parties to CONTAY return 157 & 159 Coys R.E. as location. Reported casualties to A.D.V.S. I Corps.	
"	10.5.18		Weekly conference of Div. Vet. Officer of Kitcheners area discussed.	
			Reported 203, 204, 205 F.C.R.E. & 35 Pujab G.C. Condition of animals good. Few casualties.	
			Reported to A.D.V.S. I Corps that Back Mange had further to get any positive places but been within the Div. area.	
"	11.5.18		Reported Nos. 2, 3, 9 4 Cos. 35 Div. Train. Condition of animals very fresh. Few casualties.	
"	12.5.18		Reported with remount to 106 Bdn. R.A. Few casualties & condition satisfactory.	
"	13.5.18		Reported 107 F. Amb. Condition very good.	
			" 4 W. 1st/16 & 19 W. Yorkshire. Condition satisfactory.	

WAR DIARY
INTELLIGENCE SUMMARY
(Erase heading not required.)

Army Form C. 2118.

Place	Date	Hour	Summary of Events and Information	Remarks and references to Appendices
HERISSART	14.5.18		Attended at conference of B.M.O.V.T, at 7th Div. IX Corps. Referates with of the following events:- 20.3, 20.4, 20.5 Y.G.R.E. & No.1.G.M.T.C. Few casualties & treatment satisfactory.	
"	15.5.18		Referates 159. F.A. Bde. A. Bty. Condition good. B " " " C " " " D " " " Referates distances to ammunition dumps etc. to about 5 hours in any form unhurrying & limits driving. Fires to front. Snow falling off in condition. Few hour every (Report to C.R.A.)	
"	16.5.18		Referates 157. F.A. Bde. A. Bty. forward front. A few light unused B " fires to front. Snow line of condition nearing three remnant C " very good D " good.	

Army Form C. 2118.

WAR DIARY
or
INTELLIGENCE SUMMARY.
(Erase heading not required.)

Instructions regarding War Diaries and Intelligence Summaries are contained in F. S. Regs., Part II. and the Staff Manual respectively. Title pages will be prepared in manuscript.

Place	Date	Hour	Summary of Events and Information	Remarks and references to Appendices
HERISSART	17.5.18		Inspected 106" F. Ambulance & No. 2. C.A.T.C. Condition very good. Reported onto arrival at M.V.T.	
"	18.5.18		Inspected 15' Bn. N'th'n. Cyclist. " 15" Cheshires. Condition very good. Few comments.	
"	19.5.18		Left R.A. Shelter A.V.C. O.C. 45 M.V.T. warranted visit to C.C.T at GEZAINCOURT. Took car down to H.S. M.V.T.	
"	20.5.18		Inspected visits at M.V.T. " No. 3. Indian D.A.C. Condition very good.	
			Moved to TOUTENCOURT with D.(M)V.	
TOUTENCOURT	21.5.18		Inspected 10 h. Hy. Bde. Condition present good. Two cases of gas poisoning admitted to M.V.T from 15" Cheshires. Reported to A.D.V.S. as returning to ambulances.	

WAR DIARY
or
INTELLIGENCE SUMMARY.
(Erase heading not required.)

Army Form C. 2118.

Place	Date	Hour	Summary of Events and Information	Remarks and references to Appendices
TOUTENCOURT	22.5.18		Inspected No. 1. Section 35° D.A.C.	
"	"		" " 2 " "	
"	"		" " 3 " "	
"	23.5.18		Coalition army farms. Year councillors.	
			Inspected arith to No. 1, 2, 3 & 4 hrs. Div. Trans. when Veterinary equipment.	
			Casualties, frans & treatment establ. for future. Equipment clean & complete.	
			Watched conferences of V.Gs.	
"	24.5.18		Inspected arith animals of 157° F.A. Bde.	
			Casualties ricined. On order with various Posts in B Battery.	
"	25.5.18		Inspected Veterinary equipment of the following units:—	
			106, & 107, F. Ambulances	
			Wallets & Unit hosts clean & complete.	
			Inspected arith & above units. Condition satisfactory.	
"	26.5.18		Inspected Veterinary equipments or horses of V.G.	
			attached Divisional train. Equipment clean.	
			Inspected Vet. equipments of D.T.D + 35° Imperial. Col.	
			Regimental chemming. & the animals inspected.	

WAR DIARY
or
INTELLIGENCE SUMMARY.
(Erase heading not required.)

Army Form C. 2118.

Place	Date	Hour	Summary of Events and Information	Remarks and references to Appendices
TOUTENCOURT	27.5.18		Inspected Veterinary equipment of 159th F.A. Bde. & Wallets & their chests with Depts. A.V.C. Found it slow & complete & chests deficient.	
"			Inspected Officers' chests & Wallets. Condition satisfactory.	
"			Inspected Veterinary equipment of 159th F.A. Bde. Found it slow & complete.	
"	28.5.18		Inspected Veterinary equipment of 19th Northumberland Fusiliers & found its Infantry chests movements and surgical cases, Panniers & water bottles; also corn packets Veterinary equipment to complete list.	
"			55th M.G. Corps arcte movements complete.	
"			Veterinary equipment to complete list.	
"	29.5.18		Inspected 10th Bgn. Pelve's Veterinary equipment.	
"			Inspt. 109 F.C. equipment in arcte complete & packets & ambul. tents. Chests & chests of 5 Battalions complete.	

Place	Date	Hour	Summary of Events and Information	Remarks and references to Appendices
TOUTENCOURT	30.5.18		Infantry Veterinary equipment & cob animals to the 106" & 105" Infantry Brigades. Completed the equipment when necessary. Casualties few & treatment satisfactory.	
"	31.5.18		Infantry casualties from bombs on night of 30 - 31st inst at N6.1.6 N.T.C. Proteineous bombs used. 5 Coolies killed & photograph. 2 N.D. succumbed but not seriously.	
			1. N.D. evacuated to N5" M.V.T.	
				M.V.T. Campbai Major A.V.C. D.A.D.V.S. 35 Div.

WAR DIARY of D.A.D.V.T. 35th Div.

Vol VI 1.6.18 to 30.6.18

Army Form C. 2118.

Place	Date	Hour	Summary of Events and Information	Remarks and references to Appendices
TOUTENCOURT	1.6.18		Inspected the technical & veterinary equipments & changes of 4.5" M.V.T. & completed its return movement.	
"	2.6.18		M.V. Temp. Vision E. materialized the presents to 2 bh V.E.S. Forthwith. Inspected aids animal at M.V.T. for evacuation to 2 bh V.E.S. 217H Const. Vision E. presents to 2 bh V.E.S. 2 bh V.E.S. new operating at LA VICOGNE a division of about 10 kilometers from 4.5" M.V.T. Inspected 35 Pioneer B. establishing & horses wing farm.	
"	3.6.18		Inspected ammunition carries at D.A.C. lines. 35 L.D. Whales & 7 L.D. horses. One mule totally blind & in heavy commission. D.A.C. horses report their annuals shines not wearing weighty at the turn. Instructed them to avoid on the ship or turn not the time of the shine. Animals to be closed after their mastlies & shore commands later. A.D.V.T. I bh inspected 154 & 159 F.A. Brigades & also Veterinary equipments of both Brigades. Brigades horses & mules.	

WAR DIARY
or
INTELLIGENCE SUMMARY.
(Erase heading not required.)

Army Form C. 2118.

Place	Date	Hour	Summary of Events and Information	Remarks and references to Appendices
TINCOURT	4.6.18		Inspection with armourer with 104" Sefg. Btn. & 204" W.R.E. Consultation from ammunition to treatment anti fretting". Destroyed 1. R. 35" Injured be unfit for service fractures.	
"	5.6.18		Inspection with for ammunition to 45" MVST. Consultation home with 35" D.M.C. " " front to water storing. Treatment of serious anti fretting.	
"	6.6.18		Inspection 106 & 109" F. Ambulance. Condition of animals very good. Vets equipment complete. Weekly conference of V.Os.	
"	7.6.18		9 L.D. horses & 3 L.D. Mules killed & shells, injuries in 204" F. L. R.E. on night of 6.6". 7". slight cuts. Condition of trenches not worth skimming". Inspection with armourer with 95" M.G. Corps.	

Shoeing — Wear of Shoes

WAR DIARY
INTELLIGENCE SUMMARY

Army Form C. 2118.

Place	Date	Hour	Summary of Events and Information	Remarks and references to Appendices
TOUTENCOURT	8.6.18		Inspected 35' Pigeon Ls. & 19' W. Emilium Coalition army pond.	
			Instructed O.C. 35 Pigeon Ls. to send Grey Mules "Eddie" to Field Remount Depot 3rd Army at GEZAINCOURT. (Authority D.D.R. 3rd Army.)	
	9.6.18		Inspected 106' Employ Pshn.	
			" 2th Coalition pond.	
			17' Royal Scots " "	
			12' N.Z.8 " "	
			13' N.Z.8 Coalition of horses ponds & condition of animals sent in found, but in quite good working condition.	
			Capt. R.H. Walker A.V.C. inspected for duty from Purbilie.	
	10.6.18		Inspected the following units :-	
			203, 204 & 205 F.C. R.E.	
			Condition presently good.	

Rabies
no appendix attached.

(4)

Army Form C. 2118.

WAR DIARY
or
INTELLIGENCE SUMMARY.
(Erase heading not required.)

Instructions regarding War Diaries and Intelligence Summaries are contained in F. S. Regs., Part II. and the Staff Manual respectively. Title pages will be prepared in manuscript.

Place	Date	Hour	Summary of Events and Information	Remarks and references to Appendices
TOUTENCOURT	11.6.18		Infantry Nos 1, 2, & 3 Coys. 35' Divisional Train.	
			Condition very good to fair casualties.	
			Distributed 1 Platoon belonging to 35 Brigade i.e. showing reception of Rations.	
			The care was observed during the day, & the condition of animals become worse.	
			See Appendices	
"	12.6.18		Part of train ammunition & sent to No. 13 Mobile Lab. for examination & output.	
			Infantry No 4 6. A.T.C.	
			Condition very good.	
			" in field list of armaments 7 R. 17 L.D Lorries to 1 N.D.	
			Animals ammunition & rifle are stored sorts at the front.	
"	12.6.18		Reported animals of 10's Bfn Rifles	
			15 Chasseurs, 15 Pharaonts & D. N. 11/56	
			Condition tolerable good.	
			A large proportion (about 40%) of animal in heavy sweat.	

WAR DIARY
or
INTELLIGENCE SUMMARY.
(Erase heading not required.)

Army Form C. 2118.

Place	Date	Hour	Summary of Events and Information	Remarks and references to Appendices
POUTENCOURT	14.6.19		Inspected 105' F. Ambulance at TALMAS.	
			Contributions of small parts, Evacuation, in N.B with Ulceration CELEBES to Z Corps K.G.S.	
			Veterinary equipment to equal on front inspection.	
"	15.6.19		Inspected with numbers to 105' F.Amb Rule	
			Few wounded. Treatment anti-tetanus	
			Evacuation 2 + B. Made from 15' Chalmers	
"	16.6.19		Inspected 106' + 107' F.Ambulances	
			Conditions very poor.	
			Attended to A.D.V.T.Z Where from Lieut. Smith M.V.C. attd. 106' F.Amb Rule	
			to be sent to Boots for brother training.	
BEAUQUESNE	17.6.19		Moved with D.M.V. to BEAUQUESNE.	
"	18.6.19		Inspected 106' F.Amb Rule & formulated monthly reports.	
			Conditions generally very poor. Vet. equipment complete.	
	"		H.S' M.V.G moved this morning to RAINCHEVAL.	

WAR DIARY or INTELLIGENCE SUMMARY

Army Form C. 2118.

Place	Date	Hour	Summary of Events and Information	Remarks and references to Appendices
BEAUVOISNE	19.6.18		Infantry Runner to 106' Bde Hdr R.Q. Condition satisfactory.	
"			" No. 2 Section 5' Cavalry Reserve Horse at VALVION.	
			Condition very good. Gas case reported for comment was affected with hives.	
"	20.6.18		Inspected 104' & 106' Bdys. R.C. units A.O.V.C. I.C. Hdrs. Cav. Bde. C.P. Sharpshooters A.V.C. etc. 3 C. Div horses terminated in the lines Horses to Purplemale.	
"	21.6.18		Inspected staff reinforcement from R.F. it to be returned to DIEPPE. 31 horses & 20 mules all reinspected sound & free from contagious disease. Details Temp. R.V.C. from M.V.S. to accompany these animals.	
"	22.6.18		Inspected 35' Trench bn. reinforcements monthly report on animals. Condition very good. Visits at M.S. M.V.S. for reinspection to I. bde. V.B.S.	
"	23.6.18		Inspected 14 N.D. remounts. Condition good & horses free from contagious disease.	

Army Form C. 2118.

WAR DIARY
or
INTELLIGENCE SUMMARY.
(Erase heading not required.)

Instructions regarding War Diaries and Intelligence Summaries are contained in F. S. Regs., Part II. and the Staff Manual respectively. Title pages will be prepared in manuscript.

Place	Date	Hour	Summary of Events and Information	Remarks and references to Appendices
BEAUQUESNE	24.6.18		Reported 106' Bdm. Rstn. on various counts of inputs for remount. Condition of animals generally good. Vet. equipment complete.	
"	25.6.18		Reported onto at 45' M.V.T. for inspection.	
			5. N.D. movements at 45' 6. Div. Hrs.	
"	26.6.18		Reported 35' M.D. Bde. Condition present good. Horses and country ought to flow better to BHQ.	
"	27.6.18		Reported 106', 105' & 109' Field Ambulances. Condition of animals generally good. Condition very good. Equipment complete.	
			Watched inspection of V.G.	
"	28.6.18		Reported 3. Rstn 23. 6.D. Horse & 2. N.D. movements to 35' Div. Animals from various divisions.	
"	29.6.18		Reported with movement of 45' M.V.T. for inspection to Bruen. 45' M.V.T. made orders to inspection rect of two motoring. Temp. Warrant. K. 18/16 inspects for status on 20.6.18 & is attached to 106' Fld. N.P., in relief of Staff Sergeant A.V.C. who accounts to march to Rainette for withdrawing to no Hospitalian to no. 2. V.N.	

WAR DIARY
INTELLIGENCE SUMMARY

Army Form C. 2118.

Place	Date	Hour	Summary of Events and Information	Remarks and references to Appendices
BEAUQUESNE	30.6.18		C.C. 48 M.V.S. endeavours to inform him overtime etc CANDAS at 12.50 P.M. 1.7.18. No write record transmitted to I. Corps H.Q.S.	
	1.7.18		W.O.T.P. reply Major Sun C O.i.C. 9.15.V.T. 36 Div.	

D.A.D.V.S.
35TH DIVISION.

No. 1050
1/8/18

WAR DIARY of D.A D.V.S. 35' Div.
Vol. VII
INTELLIGENCE SUMMARY. 1.7.18 to 31.7.18.

Army Form C. 2118.

Place	Date	Hour	Summary of Events and Information	Remarks and references to Appendices
BEAUQUESNE	1.7.18		Divn. left BEAUQUESNE with D.H.Q. transport at 1.30 am & marched to DULLENS & entrained to interior at about 6.15 am. Detrained at ST OMER at about 1.45 PM & marched to WIZERNES. 45" M.V.T. detrained at WIZERNES & billetted there during the night.	
WIZERNES				
OUDEZEELE	2.7.18		Marched from WIZERNES to OUDEZEELE with D.H.Q. transport & 45" M.V.T. Arrived at OUDEZEELE about 5 PM. 45" M.V.T. encamped at OUDEZEELE.	
"	3.7.18		Rode over to WINKIEZRIDGE & inspected the V.D.S. (late of attached divisions) that were reused never to be evacuated to No. 21 or V.E. Stn. located at PROVEN. Informed 45" M.V.T. veterinary Sergeants.	
"	4.7.18		Arranged to take over from 91st French Divn. the recon. of Vetinary for 45" Mobile Veterinary Section (insertion Q.11 or 2.8.) on the 6" inst.	

Army Form C. 2118.

WAR DIARY
or
INTELLIGENCE SUMMARY.
(Erase heading not required.)

Instructions regarding War Diaries and Intelligence Summaries are contained in F. S. Regs., Part II. and the Staff Manual respectively. Title pages will be prepared in manuscript.

Place	Date	Hour	Summary of Events and Information	Remarks and references to Appendices
OUDEZEELE	5.7.18		Infantry casts of 16.1.6, M.G, & 35' Trupil Gr. Few casualties to Infantry, artillery fruition. Second Major 6, came over to see V.O.& continued item that 17.4.7 would be located at Q.11.a.2.0 Shut 27. on the 6" mile.	
Q.11.a.2.0 (Sht 27)	6.7.18		4.5" M.V.T. moved to Q.11.a.2.0. Officer to O.10.v.1. handed us Q.11.a.2.0. (") Relocated 19° Northumberland Fusiliers & received monthly report to D.15.P. Conditions eng. posts & Germ casualties, the withdrew.	
"	7.7.18		Inspected the rests of 105 & 106 L. Ambulance. Casualties to a minor centine to doing satisfactory.	
"	8.7.18		Inspected 203, 204 & 205 Fd. Co. R.E. & received monthly report to D.15.T2. Infln general fever. I.R. from 204 R.E. recommended for sympathetic response. This amount amended on a unusual even month rips with an unhealthy centre.	
"	9.7.18		Attended a conference by D.A.D.V.L.'s at I Corps Sleave Question.	

Army Form C. 2118.

WAR DIARY
or
INTELLIGENCE SUMMARY.
(Erase heading not required.)

Instructions regarding War Diaries and Intelligence Summaries are contained in F. S. Regs., Part II. and the Staff Manual respectively. Title pages will be prepared in manuscript.

Place	Date	Hour	Summary of Events and Information	Remarks and references to Appendices
Q.4.a.2.0 Sheet 27	10.7.18		Infantry. 157' F.A.Bde. rendered monthly reports to D.M.V.	
			H.S.M.V.I. present permanent institution.	
			H.S.M.V.I. reports to Q.V.C. instead.	
			I Corps V.E.S. location as 1 Rifle W.G. 2 V.Y.P.E.W.G. shoots 1st Reformation from the H.S.M.V.I.	
			V.C.G. 3rd 159' F.A.Bde. reports that D. Regt. Garrison etc. 18/159/Bde. Y.A. has been recommended on 1.7.18. Officer to Officer of Bdes arrival for than	
			H.C.G. to be continued to battery whom fit.	
			Walking on other arms monthly from Walinhals; there are likely to obey any showing no draught.	
"	11.7.18		Capt. R.N. Plaskew 2.V.C. proceeded to England on 14 days leave of absence.	
			Infantry H.S.M.V.I. at Q.V.C. instead.	
			Weekly indigenous to V.G.	
			Capt. Thompson A.V.R. taken change of H.S.M.V.I. showing statement of G.C.M.Y.T.in Garrison.	
			Officers rendered to TERDEGHEM.	
TERDEGHEM	12.7.18		Infantry 15-9' F.A.Bde. & rendered monthly reports. Condition renewed & pasole. Horses very recently.	

WAR DIARY
or
INTELLIGENCE SUMMARY.
(Erase heading not required.)

Army Form C. 2118.

Instructions regarding War Diaries and Intelligence Summaries are contained in F. S. Regs., Part II. and the Staff Manual respectively. Title pages will be prepared in manuscript.

Place	Date	Hour	Summary of Events and Information	Remarks and references to Appendices
T/B DEGHEM	13.7.18		Infantry 35' D.W.C. & mounted monthly returns to D.M.D.	
			Conditions very poor.	
			Returned 6.6.45' M.G.C. to assist the horse coordination to 11 & 12 Brigades	
			Mobile Workshop for enquiries	
	14.7.18		Infantry 35' Div. Horse & mounted monthly return to D.M.D.	
			Conditions very poor & horses in condition.	
			Temp. A.V.C. returned for duty with 35' M.F.hosp. (Temp White A.V.C.)	
	15.7.18		Infantry 10.6' Bdgs. Bde.	
			12'N.F.F. very poor, 10'N.F.F. & 17' Royal Scots poor. Remounts monthly return to I.V.E.S.	
	16.7.18		Infantry visits at 45' M.V.C. for examination to I & 6.2 Mobile Workshop for enquiries.	
			Horses Ambulance sent to 11& 6.2 Mobile Workshop for enquiries.	
	17.7.18		Infantry 10'H' Infantry Bde.	
			Condition to 10'Z.F. Scrap. 17'Z.F. general good. 2.9 horses and four	
			19'D.F.F. poor. 15'H poor. Work a hand & given showing present acute conditions	
			is very heavy. Rations on taken at showing the complete.	
			Arrived out from 6 to 7 horses. Rendered monthly return for this Brigade.	

(5)

Army Form C. 2118.

WAR DIARY
or
INTELLIGENCE SUMMARY.
(Erase heading not required.)

Instructions regarding War Diaries and Intelligence Summaries are contained in F. S. Regs., Part II. and the Staff Manual respectively. Title pages will be prepared in manuscript.

Place	Date	Hour	Summary of Events and Information	Remarks and references to Appendices
TARDEGHEM	18.7.18		Infantie 10.5" F. Ambulance constitute army pool, and at 4.5" M.V.T. for evacuation to I hr V.E.S.	
"	19.7.18		Infantie 10.5" Bdy, Bde, constitute friendly pool. Evacuation mostly infant to B.T.D. Arrival our prisoners check work, mostly at night from D.30 p.m. to 3.30 a.m.	
			Recommended that the above system be supplemented by some feeding arrangement.	
"	20.7.18		Infantie with us 4.5" M.V.T. for evacuation to I hr V.E.S.	
"	21.7.18		Infantie with us 35" D.A.C. Few casualties & technical entertainmt.	
"	22.7.18		Attached companies to D,19,24.V.T at I hr N.Q. The following subjects were discussed:— (1) Standard to cover for keeping horses at work in the fields. (2) Clothing (Method to be adopted.) 16 men expected to establish a central helping station.	

A6945 Wt. W1142/M1160 350,000 12/16 D. D. & L. Forms/C./2118/14.

WAR DIARY
or
INTELLIGENCE SUMMARY.
(Erase heading not required.)

Army Form C. 2118.

Place	Date	Hour	Summary of Events and Information	Remarks and references to Appendices
TERDEGHEM.	23.7.18.		Weary man showing the day. Firing away every Lewis gun ammunition transports.	
"	24.7.18		Inspection carts at M.V.1. for ammunition to 5 Corps N.E.S. Inspection 35" M.T. Coys.	
			Inspection previously given. Remounts report to D.A.D.R. 20 Coys of Remounts later received in M.V.1. for distribution to units.	
"	25.7.18		Inspection 105 F. Ambulance. Inspection any good. Worked conference by V.G.	
"	26.7.18		Inspection 106 F. Ambulance at WEMAERS-CAPPEL. Inspection any good.	
"	27.7.18		Inspection 107 Fd. Ambulance & 19' M. Fd. Ambulance to both units army good. Inspection with Lt. Col. 35" Hospital lus. at four intermediate stations in evacuation.	
"	28.7.18		Capt. McArthur A.V.C. reports from Rouen. Inspection carts at M.V.1. for ammunition to E Corps N.E.S.	

Army Form C. 2118.

WAR DIARY
or
INTELLIGENCE SUMMARY.
(Erase heading not required.)

Instructions regarding War Diaries and Intelligence Summaries are contained in F. S. Regs., Part II. and the Staff Manual respectively. Title pages will be prepared in manuscript.

Place	Date	Hour	Summary of Events and Information	Remarks and references to Appendices
TERDEGHEM	28.7.18		50 Feb to 6. Australian Flash regiment R.V.N. arms rivaled to send b. to quin home, & end batting of 157 F.A.Bde. V.6 in order to get them into new batteries, also flats to be continued with numbers where in our & intended to this officers together with a report as to their suitability or otherwise.	
"	29.7.18.		Ammunition A.D.V.S I corps at less ammunition at 12, 13, C, & D/159 F.A.Bde.y A,C & D 157 F.A.Bde. A.D.V.S. I Corps visited 45 M.V.T. Pte. Thurst M.A. recommended to M.A./C.S. in please of CPL Wentworth 45 M.V.T. transferred to Reg.B.1.V.C in filled units promotion from 11.7.18. Reports 25 Injured C.a. & remainder monthly outputs.	
"	30.7.18		Condition very poor. Injuries to the following animals:- 15" Shrapnel : gunnante 1. H.D. mill Shrapnel Cf. Petersham + 1. Rider unit. Inspective mounts. three animal sent as remounts. Inspected 19" F.P. & remounts. 1. H.D. for debility.	

Army Form C. 2118.

WAR DIARY
or
INTELLIGENCE SUMMARY.
(Erase heading not required.)

Instructions regarding War Diaries and Intelligence Summaries are contained in F. S. Regs., Part II. and the Staff Manual respectively. Title pages will be prepared in manuscript.

Place	Date	Hour	Summary of Events and Information	Remarks and references to Appendices
TERDEGHEM	21.7.18		29.7.18. A.D.V.S. I Corps confirm 159 F.A. Orders to report to A.B.C. Batteries in front worth while condition that B. batting as an open requisition is movement order. G.C. 159 F.A. Bde reports to 35 Div. O. that the animals in unit from leaving from G_____ tired to inspect which is the only company available in order for meals. A complete 6 audit is also sent. I find that it continues to keep account of expense weather or remounts. 2000 horses from to field battle. Report that sick and unite coughs to be awaiting of similar sick horses of the Dn unable to be Blacksmith simply movements that as occurrence of _____	
			1.8.18	
			W.W. Tomplet Major A.V.C	
			A.D.V.S. 35th Div.	

D.A.D.V.S.
85TH DIVISION
Army Form C. 2118.
No. 124
Date 1/9/18

WAR DIARY of D.A.D.V.S. 35th Div.
or
INTELLIGENCE SUMMARY. Vol VIII 1.8.16 to 31.8.16

(Erase heading not required.)

Vol 31

Place	Date	Hour	Summary of Events and Information	Remarks and references to Appendices
TERDEGHEM	1.8.18		Inspected 90th Infantry Bde, 30th Div. attended. Inspected 26 Bde Mobilization games. 2/15 London Rgt " Give to from. 2/14 & 2/16 London Rgt – Corporals. Work on animals is carried on mostly shown at night. Weekly conference at V.G.	
"	2.8.18	6.0	Inspected 26.6.0 horses from D/159 F.A.Bde sent back to We 2. Pushing D.V.A.C. for a rest & in order to improve their condition. The majority of them were in poor condition, but could be little cont. with animal condition.	
"	3.8.18		Inspected 27th Cumbrian Rfn. mobilization of magnif. army farm. aids of 17 & 18 Lancashire Fusiliers. Inoculated animals with slight reaction.	
"	4.8.18		Arranged for 25 M.V.S.T. to escort to horses inoculated at 9.14 a.9.9. Commence to Terdeghem all ammunic. Inspected 26 horses sent to DAC. from D/159 Rd F.A. with D.ADMS. These are unfit on account of their condition.	

WAR DIARY
or
INTELLIGENCE SUMMARY.
(Erase heading not required.)

Army Form C. 2118.

Place	Date	Hour	Summary of Events and Information	Remarks and references to Appendices
TERDEGHEM	4.9.18		D.A.D.V.S. 30' Div called & inspected units of 4.5" M.V.T. awaiting to continue to Tatinghem with the new postion.	
"	5.9.18		Inspected our billets & 4.5" M.V.T. Ly at Q.14.a.9.9. Phot 27. & with linen for ammunition to Torpinlets.	
"	6.9.18		Proceeded on leave to ENGLAND from 7th to 21st August. Capt. R.H. Stalker A.V.C. to do duty during absence on leave.	
"	7.9.18		Inspection 55" D.A.C. with A.D.V.S. I Corps.	
"	8.9.18		V.O. Brought those wanted A.V.C.A. Sergts to their Offices.	
"	9.9.18		Attended conference D.V.D.V.S. at I Corps N.Q.	
CASSELL	10.9.18		D.A.D.S. ammended to CASSELL.	
"	11.9.18		Miniquento to unit up into the line. Inspection 203rd F.C. R.E.	
"	12.9.18		Lyt. Bruckard reported to 131/159. F.A. Pele. for duty. 4.5" M.V.T. moved to R.13.b.3.5. Phot 27.	
"	13.9.18		Inspection 35' Dev. Repair C. Castilian Farewell Parade.	

WAR DIARY or INTELLIGENCE SUMMARY

Army Form C. 2118.

Place	Date	Hour	Summary of Events and Information	Remarks and references to Appendices
CASSEL	14.8.18		Infantry 106" Infantry Bde.	
"	15.8.18		Instants of seven artil. fortany. Infantry 10th Infantry 13de.	
"	16.8.18		Instants of seven artil. fortany. Infantry 15.9.2.8.13de.	
"	17.8.18		Tark made trials downs artil. fortany.	
"	18.8.18		Infantry IX was for conversation at 45 M.V.T. 3.5" M.V. Corps. Tank ever working artif. fatany purposes.	
"	19.8.18		Examined elements at 35 D.A.C. All appointed from Corps writing on drivers.	
"	20.8.18		Infantry No.1 L. Div. Corps. Intended them to do so. No lorry arms in use.	
"	21.8.18		Infantry of people mens.	
"	22.8.18		Returned from leave & resumed duties of D.A.O.V.T.	

WAR DIARY
or
INTELLIGENCE SUMMARY.
(Erase heading not required.)

Army Form C. 2118.

Place	Date	Hour	Summary of Events and Information	Remarks and references to Appendices
CASSELL	23.8.18		Inspected D/159, F.A. Bde. Condition of harness & battery Guns, ammunition, bookbinders generally good. Limbers & harness that had not made recent improvements.	
"	24.8.18		Inspected 157 F.A. Bde. with 6-L Brigadier. A Bty present good; ammunition as fair to poor condition only. B " 50% fair to good. C " 50% fair to poor. D battery fair to good. Received monthly report to D.A.D. from this brigade.	
"	25.8.18		Inspected 17 F. Howitzers. Condition fair to good. 2 horses unsuitable for Gun condition. There is room to extend its work there to establish more hope; 15 unserviceable gave horse in this lines. Inspected 20 horses to D/159 F.A. Bde. on arrival (Fielding). Condition fair but unfair to be uninspiring. Applied to A.D.V.S. help for improvement of unserviceable more ones from this battery.	

WAR DIARY
or
INTELLIGENCE SUMMARY.
(Erase heading not required.)

Army Form C. 2118.

Place	Date	Hour	Summary of Events and Information	Remarks and references to Appendices
CHSEL	26.8.18		Imputed 159" F.A. Bde.	
			A. Bty personal posts in condition	
			B. " " " "	
			C. " " " " about 20 animals fair to good.	
			D. " " condition fair to good. Harness improvements	
			Bombards monthly report to Gen. G.O.R.E.P., on Chris transpire.	
"	27.8.18		Imputed 203" F.L. R.E.	
			condition personal good, transportation & R's for stability & 1 L.D for stricture	
			" 35" Pipil Cs. condition good.	
			" with 45" M.V.1. for evacuation to hospital.	
"	28.8.18		Imputed 19 Bhn D.T.F.	
			condition personal good. A few animals not fair to good.	
			Lenes ment to currently close to cent arms.	
"	29.8.18		A.D.V.S. I Corps inspected the horses of	
			A, B, C & D Batteries 159" F.A. Bde.	
			Verbal endorsement of V.G. by the Division	

WAR DIARY
or
INTELLIGENCE SUMMARY.
(Erase heading not required.)

Army Form C. 2118.

Place	Date	Hour	Summary of Events and Information	Remarks and references to Appendices
CASSEL	30.9.18		Inspected 18' T.T. condition of animals generally good. " on site for a clipping station at 9.20. C.6.5. sheet 27 & inspected it. suitable for the purpose.	
"	31.9.18		Inspected 35' Supply C. Condition generally good. New annexation. Veterinary equipment complete.	

W.T. Taylor Major A.V.C.
9.10.18. T. 35" Div.

D.A.D.V.S.
Army Form C. 2118
35TH DIVISION.
No. 1439
Date 3/10/18

WAR DIARY of D.A.D.V.S. 35th Div.
Vol. IX.
INTELLIGENCE SUMMARY 1.9.18 to 30.9.18.
(Erase heading not required.)

Vol 32

Instructions regarding War Diaries and Intelligence Summaries are contained in F. S. Regs., Part II. and the Staff Manual respectively. Title pages will be prepared in manuscript.

Place	Date	Hour	Summary of Events and Information	Remarks and references to Appendices
CASSEL	1.9.18		Inspected milk recounts at H.S. M.V.T. for evacuation to hospitals. 2 Klim vans for 105" F.Amb. & 2.4 R.E. respectively received by train. Ambulance M.V.T. to be ready to move.	
MERREELE	2.9.18		Moved with D.H.Q. to MERREELE, now attached to 2nd Corps. H.S. M.V.T. located at " Inspected 203" F. & R.E. & H.S. 2 C. Div. Train. Condition of animals satisfactory.	
"	3.9.18		Visited A.D.V.S. 2nd Corps at Corps H.Q. V/Lt. Astley. W. (A.V.C.) reported for duty in relief of A/V/Lt. Whyte (A.V.C.) proceeded in command in reserve Corps.	
VOGELTJE	4.9.10		Moved with D.H.Q. to VOGELTJE. H.S. M.V.T. moved to 29/L.10 a.3.0.	
"	5.9.18		Inspected 78 Remounts arrived on 4.9.18 from CALAIS by road. all apparently free from contagious diseases. H.S. M.V.T. at new billets. Weekly conference of V.Os.	

Army Form C. 2118.

WAR DIARY
or
INTELLIGENCE SUMMARY.
(Erase heading not required.)

Instructions regarding War Diaries and Intelligence Summaries are contained in F. S. Regs. Part II. and the Staff Manual respectively. Title pages will be prepared in manuscript.

Place	Date	Hour	Summary of Events and Information	Remarks and references to Appendices
VOGELTJE	6.9.18		Inspected No 1 & 2 Autumn D.A.C. Condition good & Vet. equipment complete.	
"			" 105" Hy. Bde. Condition very good. Rendered monthly report to D.M.S.	
"			" 4.5" M.V.I. in main billets at Bleu Camp. At front positions & accommodation for M.V.I.	
"	7.9.18		Inspected 106" Infantry Bde. Condition generally good. Rendered monthly report to D.M.S.	
"	8.9.18		Inspected 3.5" Ropid C. Condition generally good. Inspected sick at 4.5" M.V.I.	
"	9.9.18		Inspected D Battery 15 y P.A.Bde. Many animal still in light condition.	
"			" D Battery 15 y P.A.Bde. Animals gone to front, but there is a great marked improvement. Accomplished A.V. & O.M.G. to men in advance to inspect transport lines with a view to finding standings nearer the front line. Location in Gun standings without overhead cover.	

Army Form C. 2118.

WAR DIARY
or
INTELLIGENCE SUMMARY.
(Erase heading not required.)

Instructions regarding War Diaries and Intelligence Summaries are contained in F. S. Regs., Part II. and the Staff Manual respectively. Title pages will be prepared in manuscript.

Place	Date	Hour	Summary of Events and Information	Remarks and references to Appendices
VOGELTJE	10.9.18		Inspected the 104th Infantry Bde. T. and sent monthly report to D.N.Q. 18" I. R.: Condition any poor. 19" I. R.: " " " fair to good. 19" D.I.B. " " " good. General made up in fair condition. The majority of animals are under cover. Attended a conference of D.A.D.V.S. at II Corps N.Q.	
"	11.9.18		Accompanied A.D.V.S. II Corps around the transport lines of the following units:— 106" Infantry Bde. 104 " " 203, 204, & 205 Co. R.E. 105" Infantry Bde. & 4.5" Mobile Veterinary Section. Inspected 106 F. Ambulance transport. Condition very good. Standing in the open. Inspected transport of 35 M.J. Coy. Condition generally good. Four animals of a minor nature. Went on forward to V. Cr.	
"	12.9.18			
"	13.9.18		Inspected B/159 F.A. Bde. Condition fair to good. Later eaten, however in condition. Inspected 3 horses of C/159 F.A. Bde. with internal trouble, probably due to forage. Inspected oats & hay. Oats were of poor quality.	

Army Form C. 2118.

WAR DIARY
or
INTELLIGENCE SUMMARY.
(Erase heading not required.)

Instructions regarding War Diaries and Intelligence Summaries are contained in F. S. Regs., Part II. and the Staff Manual respectively. Title pages will be prepared in manuscript.

Place	Date	Hour	Summary of Events and Information	Remarks and references to Appendices
VOGELTJE	14.9.18		Inspected sick animals at 25' M.V.I. for evacuation to hospital. Weather wet. Further very unsettly.	
"	15.9.18		Inspected W.S. Picton D.A.C. Condition very poor. Veterinary equipment complete & serviceable.	
"	16.9.18		Inspected 203rd, 204, 205' F. Co. R.E. Condition personnel good. 13.4.D. Horses in 204 R.E. in light condition. Veterinary equipment complete & serviceable.	
WARATAH FARM	17.9.18		D.H.Q. moved to WARATAH FARM 28/ G.15.a.6.0. Inspected transport of 104' F. Ambulance. Condition very poor. Veterinary equipment complete & serviceable.	
"	18.9.18		Inspected No. 1, 2, & 3 Section D.A.C. sick animals. All minor cases & doing satisfactorily.	
"	19.9.18		Inspected 105' F. Ambulance. Condition good. Veterinary equipment complete & serviceable.	

WAR DIARY or INTELLIGENCE SUMMARY

Army Form C. 2118.

(Erase heading not required.)

Place	Date	Hour	Summary of Events and Information	Remarks and references to Appendices
WARATAH FARM 29/G.15.a.6.0	20.9.18		45" M.V.T. moved to 29/G.9.b.2.8. Inspected new billets & met A.D.V.S. XII Corps at the 17.V.T. Visited the transport lines of 104', 105', & 106' Bdys. Bdes. Majority of animals grazing in the vicinity of their lines.	
"	21.9.18		45" M.V.T. moved to 20/G.16.a.6.3 ZEALAND FARM. Inspected 35' Trepine Co. Condition present good.	
"	22.9.18		Inspected D/157 F.A.Bde. Condition fair to good. Many 25% of horses, remainder good. Animals in the open. XV.Div. Condition have improved. " 35' Div. train. Under shelter except for No. 3.Co. which is in the open. Condition generally very good.	
"	23.9.18		Inspected mule convoys at 45" M.V.T. Visited the transport lines & inspected the sick animals, of 105'Hy.Bde, 35'Trepine Co.	
"	24.9.18		Inspected 157 F.A.Bde & rendered monthly report to D.M.S. Condition generally good.	

WAR DIARY or INTELLIGENCE SUMMARY

Army Form C. 2118.

Place	Date	Hour	Summary of Events and Information	Remarks and references to Appendices
WARATAH	25.9.18		Inspected 159 F.A. Bde. + rendered monthly report for same. A, B, + C. Batteries present. D. Battery gone to pren. All animals in the open. Received instruction from A.D.V.S. XIX Corps to evacuate sick animals to VII Corps V.E.S. located at 27/L.29.a.3.5.	
"	26.9.18		Inspected 35 Bgn. M.T. Corps + rendered report to D.V.P. Condition generally good. Sick animals noted 203, 204 + 205 Y. L. R.E. Evacuate I.R with Resp. Neumo from 204 Coy. Other men of a slight nature. Placed monthly conference of Veterinary Officers.	
"	27.9.18		Inspected sick animals at 45 M.V.S. for evacuation to 7 Corps V.E.S. Visited detachment 10 Bgn. Canadian Rly Troops. No casualties amongst the Mules.	
"	28.9.18		Visited the transport of following units:— 203, 204, 205 Cos R.E. 19 M.F + 105 Coy Pnrs. Found on site for 45 M.V.S. at 20/N.8.d.5.9.	

Army Form C. 2118.

WAR DIARY
or
INTELLIGENCE SUMMARY.
(Erase heading not required.)

Instructions regarding War Diaries and Intelligence Summaries are contained in F.S. Regs., Part II. and the Staff Manual respectively. Title pages will be prepared in manuscript.

Place	Date	Hour	Summary of Events and Information	Remarks and references to Appendices
WARATAH FARM.	29.9.18		45th M.V.T. moved to 28/H.8.d.5.9. Inspected the work of 104, 105, 106 Indyn. Rns. 14 animals evacuated on 28 + 29 for sickness. Weather very hot.	
ASSAM.	30.9.18		Moved to ASSAM FARM with D.M.9 at H.22.a.2.7. Formed an advanced Veterinary Post at 28/H.24 Centrals. Weather continues to be very wet. Majority of animals in the open. Road very bad for transport.	

W.M.Taylor, Major A.V.C.
D.A.D.V.S. 35 Div.

Army Form C. 2118.

WAR DIARY of D.A.D.V.T. 35th Div.
Vol. V
INTELLIGENCE SUMMARY. 1.10.18 to 31.10.18

(Erase heading not required.)

No 34

Place	Date	Hour	Summary of Events and Information	Remarks and references to Appendices
ASSAM FARM D/H 22.a.2.7	1.10.18		Route from ZILLEBEKE to ZANDVOORDE. Roads very rough & broken; very difficult for wheel transport. All roads under repair. Inspected 203, 204 & 205 Co. R.E. Boertie proper; No 6 Infy. Bde.; Brestin present front. All animals in the open.	
"	2.10.18		Visited the lines of 104, 105 & 106 Infy. Bdes. at various mounted lines, through GHELUVELT on YPRES-MENIN RD. Moved through HOOGE, very bad, but other parts in better condition. 45th M.A.C. moved to DOHL'S HOUSE. 28/I.19.b central. Advanced post I.17.a.9.9.	
"	3.10.18		All transport withdrawn from the line. Inspected the following units:— 105, & 106 Bdes. RFA., 55 Repair Co. L. Battery 157 Bde. R.F.A. Mostly animals generally prove considering the hard work & bad weather.	

Army Form C. 2118.

WAR DIARY
or
INTELLIGENCE SUMMARY.
(Erase heading not required.)

Instructions regarding War Diaries and Intelligence
Summaries are contained in F. S. Regs., Part II.
and the Staff Manual respectively. Title pages
will be prepared in manuscript.

Place	Date	Hour	Summary of Events and Information	Remarks and references to Appendices
ASSAM FARM. 2D/N22.a.2.7	4.9.18 10		Infantes 157 Bde R.F.A. A, B, C, Btys. locations prom. D Bty location failed to prove. " 104 Hy. Bde. locations prove prov.	
"	5.9.18 10		Infantes 5.5 Howrs (Plements) 30 29 moved to D/157 Bde R.F.A. 28 " " " to 35 M.y. b/w. 5 N.D. to Div. Hum. locations prove prove	
"	6.9.18 10		Infantes nil amount at 45 M.V.T. for examination.	
"	7.9.18 10		Infantes 159 4.F.A. Bde. All animals in the flour. locations prove prove. V.Co 157 F.A.Bde reports 24 horses killed & 19 wounded by bombing last night; of the latter evacuated to M.V.T. Strongpoint stable for 10.2 wounds arrived of wounds from enemy S.	
"	10 8.9.18		Infantes 102 Plements. All amount apparently free from disease except for one case of Ringworm in a mule. Infantes nile amount at 45 M.V.T.	

Army Form C. 2118.

WAR DIARY
or
INTELLIGENCE SUMMARY.
(Erase heading not required.)

Instructions regarding War Diaries and Intelligence Summaries are contained in F. S. Regs., Part II. and the Staff Manual respectively. Title pages will be prepared in manuscript.

Place	Date	Hour	Summary of Events and Information	Remarks and references to Appendices
ASSAM FARM	9.10.18		Reported to Mules belonging to 15th Br Cheshire Regt. Animals exhausted. M. Mulavan alternate from effects of some irritants. Probably mustard gas inspite with gross of other fodder. Evacuated two of them animals to D.A.D.V.S. at Corps H.Q. attached in conference to D.A.D.V.S.	
"	10.10.18		Reported 35th D.A.C. Condition very poor. All animals in the open. " 106 F. Ambulance Condition very poor. Attended in the open. Watch entrance of V.G.	
"	11.10.18		Reported with to 35th Division. Various consultation + visiting vets. frontwt. Been busy with 10th N.Z.F. + evacuated its to M.V.T. 2 mules with symptoms effects with mustard gas, ie 15th Cheshires. Gave opium to the remaining. " the Detachment at the unknown part of 45th M.V.T.	
"	12.10.18		Reported 30 Remounts in 15th L.D. German & 15th L.D. Mules. Condition generally poor + apparently free from disease.	

(3)

WAR DIARY
or
INTELLIGENCE SUMMARY

Army Form C. 2118.

Place	Date	Hour	Summary of Events and Information	Remarks and references to Appendices
ASS'N FARM	13.10.18		Moved advance punt to 45˚M.V.1 to CLAPHAM JUNCTION. 28I J 13 d. 9. 9. Infanta with us 45˚M.V.1. for mountain to V.E.S.	
"	14.10.18		35˚Div. advance through MOUSSELE. 12 wounded animals situated at Advance Post during the morning.	
"	15.10.18		Visited transport lines of 104,106 & 106˚ Infy Bdes & 204,203,205 R.E. in forward area. Selected a site for 45˚M.V.1. beyond GHELUVELT. Infanta at Advance Post at CLAPHAM-JUNCTION.	
"	16.10.18		45˚M.V.1. moved to Phut 28/K 26 d.4.9. Met party with 100 animals at Poperinghe & arranged billets for the night. Impatas animals & sent them apparently from chessar with mountain. I Made mention of Mange. Animals will proceed to D.M.C. at GHELUVELT tomorrow morning. Distance from 45˚M.V.1. to V.E.S. is now about 19 kilometres for complete journey.	

WAR DIARY or INTELLIGENCE SUMMARY

Army Form C. 2118.

Place	Date	Hour	Summary of Events and Information	Remarks and references to Appendices
ASSAM FARM	17/10/18		Found 100 dismounts to units of Division. Visited 45" M.V.S. & imputate stn with wounded for evacuation.	
POESELHOEK	18/10/18		Moved with D.H.Q. to POESELHOEK L.26.c D.9. sheet 28.	
"	19/10/18		Reported C + D Batteries 159 Bde R.F.A. Condition present good. C Battery 157 Bde B.F.A. " " " E Battery 157 Bde B.F.A. " " " Work has been carried on from. Plenty of margin handy. 45" M.V.S. moved to POESELHOEK. 7 V.E.S moved to 28/L.14.d.0.4. & open on 21.10.18.	
"	20.10.18		Arranged for an Advanced post of M.V.S at M.S. B.9.g.9. E4 Ruine Fm. M.V.1 then started for work for evacuation. Horse ambulance to turn down.	
MARCKE	21.10.18		Moved with D.H.Q. to MARCKE. Imputate B. Battery 159 Bde R.F.A. Condition present good.	

Army Form C. 2118.

WAR DIARY
or
INTELLIGENCE SUMMARY.
(Erase heading not required.)

Instructions regarding War Diaries and Intelligence Summaries are contained in F. S. Regs., Part II. and the Staff Manual respectively. Title pages will be prepared in manuscript.

Place	Date	Hour	Summary of Events and Information	Remarks and references to Appendices
MARCKE	22/10/18		Reinforced 159 Bde. R.F.A. with 6.6 Brigade. A.B. build's posn. C. 1145 V.mg. posn. D. Rly. ground posn: is four minutes in Light Condition. 4.5 M.V.T. moved to. 29/N. M.6. G.h.D. near MARCKE.	
"	23/10/18		N.D.v.1 VII in situ – 4.5" M.V.T. Reinforced 159. Bde. R.F.A. A. & C. Btys. inaction posn. B. in my posn. D. ground posn. into a possible questioning in depth condition.	
COURTRAI	24/10/18		Moved with D.H.Q. to 47 Rue de Tournay de Tournai. Reinforced 203, 204, & 205. Co. R.E. Location ground posn. 203, ? 204 for Water shelter. Weekly conference of K.G.s. 7 men of 9 Division detached during the month & Units & M.V.T.	
"	25/10/18		Reinforced 100 remounts. All equipment from 7pm strain, 105" 4" Antitank & 19 Methodical Machines. Leaders to remount my posn.	

Army Form C. 2118.

WAR DIARY
or
INTELLIGENCE SUMMARY.
(Erase heading not required.)

Place	Date	Hour	Summary of Events and Information	Remarks and references to Appendices
COURTRAI	26.10.18		Inspected 106" & 109" F. Ambulances & ordered monthly reports for these units. Arranged on new form evacuation. Inspected sick at M.V.1 for evacuation to V.E.S.	
"	27.10.18		Maj. Watson A.V.C. arrived for evacuation to Divn. on account of unfit illness. Instructed him to M/F to A.V.C. Records. Arranged for 45" M.V.S. to move to SWEVEGHEM. All transport moving forward. Deployment also moving forward this evening.	
SWEVEGHEM	28.10.18		Moved into B.H.Q. to SWEVEGHEM. 45" M.V.1 moved to " . T.V.E.S moved to BISSEGHEM on COURTRAI ROAD. Inspected 104" Fd. Ambs. Ration & evacuation arrangements & conditions generally good. 27 horses killed & 1 bull wounded & one bomb (enemy) + 2 horses killed by a shell; animals belongs to 35" Imperial Co.	
"	29.10.18		Inspected 105" F.Amb. Ration 15" Divnl. Employment & M. Staffs any parn. 15" Clothing Coron. Received monthly reports.	

Army Form C. 2118.

WAR DIARY
or
INTELLIGENCE SUMMARY.
(Erase heading not required.)

Instructions regarding War Diaries and Intelligence Summaries are contained in F. S. Regs., Part II. and the Staff Manual respectively. Title pages will be prepared in manuscript.

Place	Date	Hour	Summary of Events and Information	Remarks and references to Appendices
SWEVEGHEM.	30.10.18		Inspected B & D Coys. 35" M.T. Corps. Condition of men & mules good. D. Coy under cover. A sick animal at H.S. M.V.S.	
"	31.10.18		5" F.A. horses killed & 5 H.D. wounded + chill foin, belonging to D.Coy. Casualties removed since midnight. Infected mules at H.S. M.V.T. No. 3. Dutch D.A.C. Condition very good.	

W. M. Temple. Major. A.V.C.
D.A.D.V.S. 35" Div.

Army Form C. 2118.

WAR DIARY of D.A.D.V.S. 35' Div.
INTELLIGENCE SUMMARY.
Vol. XI
(Erase heading not required.) 1.11.18 to 30.11.18

Place	Date	Hour	Summary of Events and Information	Remarks and references to Appendices
SWEVEGHEM	1.11.18		Inspected 17' Royal Scots & 12' N.F.A. Arrived forty mule issues: Candidate from " 204 F.C.R.E. & innocula 1. L.D for "Debility". Candidate passed generally. " 203" F.C.R.E. Candidate passed. Majority of innocula were rather debilitated.	
"	2.11.18		Arranged for A.D.V.S. XV Corps to inspect horses on 6' 157 & 159 Brdes. R.F.A on Wednesday 6' Nov. Inst. Inspected about 200 mules, Canish B/C	the Premises at SWEVEGHEM as to their suitability for accommodation on ; convalescent park. With result out of the three.	
"	3.11.18		Inspected mules at M.V.T. wounded B 108' Vete M.D. Evacuation park.	
"	4.11.18		Inspected horses of 105' F. Ambulance. Candidate any good. Inspected mules wounded at 35' M.V.S.	

Army Form C. 2118.

WAR DIARY
or
INTELLIGENCE SUMMARY.
(Erase heading not required.)

Instructions regarding War Diaries and Intelligence Summaries are contained in F. S. Regs., Part II. and the Staff Manual respectively. Title pages will be prepared in manuscript.

Place	Date	Hour	Summary of Events and Information	Remarks and references to Appendices
SWEVEGHEM	5.11.18		Wagon lines of D. Artillery + D.H.C. moved forward last night & this morning. Advanced H.Q. of 45" M.V.1 established at 29/O.6 a 5.2. Weather very wet.	
"	6.11.18		Enquiries 1 & 2 Futuro D.H.C. Entire regiment. All armouries in the open. D/157 Bde R.F.A. amounts to 2 rounds for Debility. 15 /6 . 6 rounds in Battery, in light condition. D/159 Bde R.F.A. Condition poorly fed. Weather continues wet.	
ST. LOUIS.	7.11.18		Moved with D.H.Q. to ST. LOUIS. Waiting influence of V.G.	
"	8.11.18		Inspection with armouries at 45" M.V.1. Arrange for M.V.1 to move near ST. LOUIS tomorrow.	

Army Form C. 2118.

(3)

WAR DIARY
or
INTELLIGENCE SUMMARY.

(Erase heading not required.)

Instructions regarding War Diaries and Intelligence Summaries are contained in F.S. Regs., Part II. and the Staff Manual respectively. Title pages will be prepared in manuscript.

Place	Date	Hour	Summary of Events and Information	Remarks and references to Appendices
ST. LOUIS.	9.11.18		Attended a conference to D.A.O.S.V.7 at XIX Corps. 45" M.V.7 moved to 29/I 34 a.9.9.9. 50 Remount arrived at Maulde. Arranged for O.C. 45" M.V.7 to inspect them. Weather warm and fine.	
"	10.11.18		Issued 50 remounts at Railhead to Lupid, horse, 10's & 11's 6" Hows.	
QUAREMONT	11.11.18		45" M.V.7 moved to QUAREMONT. 29/W.4 a. Entire. Notified at movement. A.D.V.7 XIX Corps intimates that 7 V.E.7 is moving to VICHTE on 12.11.18. Headquarters Moved with BMD. to QUAREMONT. Armistice to take effect from 11 am.	
"	12.11.18		45" M.V.7 established an Advanced Post at 30/S.11 QUARTA-VENTS 9. Inspected 157" Bde R.F.A. A, B & C Batteries passing fit. D Battery about 12/% at light condition, others passed power. 10 animals noted for evacuation.	

D.D. & L., London, E.C.
(A10266) Wt. W. 1300/P713 750,000 2/16 Sch. 52 Forms/C2118/16

Army Form C. 2118.

WAR DIARY
or
INTELLIGENCE SUMMARY.
(Erase heading not required.)

Place	Date	Hour	Summary of Events and Information	Remarks and references to Appendices
QUAREMONT	13.11.18		Inspected 204 & 205 Field Co. R.E. Condition improved and horses 1 L.D. from 204 R.E. for Debility & 1 L.D. from 205 R.E. for sore shoulder of withers.	
"	14.11.18		Weekly inspection of V.C.	
"	15.11.18		Inspected animals of 115" Infantry Bde. 4" N. Staffs. Condition very good. Animals under cover. 15. Cheshires " " " " 15. Notts & Derbys " " " "	
"	16.11.18		Inspected No.1. L.G.M.G.C. 105" L. Ambulance Condition of animals good. Veterinary equipment complete & serviceable.	
"	17.11.18		Inspected units for remounts at H.S.M.V.T. Arranged for H.S.M.V.T. to proceed to HARLEBEKE on 18.11.18.	

WAR DIARY or INTELLIGENCE SUMMARY.

Army Form C. 2118.

Place	Date	Hour	Summary of Events and Information	Remarks and references to Appendices
HARLEBEKE	18.11.18		Removed to HARLEBEKE with D.M.P.	
"	19.11.18	1.30 p.m.	Arrived at HARLEBEKE 1.30 p.m. & found men which lay outside some former stable number "RAUDÉ". Installed them into these stable which were put ready to house them. Arranged for men more under supervision to H.S M.W.1 to have their Final Disinfection.	
"	20.11.18		Inspection 11. R. & 16. L. D. hour for transfer to another Infirmary from 35 Div. Ashurst	
"	21.11.18		Inspection 9/(15) Bde. R.F.A. & reinoculated 6 animals for "Debility" Ashurst ready horse. Inspection 35 Divn Tn. 35 Div Artillery for transfer to 2nd Ech: with 1st at H.S. M.W.1 for inoculation to V.E.S.	

WAR DIARY or INTELLIGENCE SUMMARY

Army Form C. 2118.

Place	Date	Hour	Summary of Events and Information	Remarks and references to Appendices
HARLEBEKE	22.11.18.		Infantry Details of the following Brigades having a total of 632 animals:- 152, 160 Bdes. R.F.A.; 34th Division. 187, 190 " " ; 41st Division. 11th Army Field Artillery Bde. monty transported 116 animals each to 45" M.V.T. for their Phisicians, ability example for a dinner & Veterinary attendance on these animals.	
"	23.11.18.		Infantry nil & 35th Infored w. & there for examination at 45" M.V.T.	
"	24.11.18.		Infantry Details to 34 & 41st Div. Artillery & 11th A.F.A Bde. Examined 10 animals each to 45" M.V.T. Marched 14 & 19 animals from whom details to 35 Div. (entirely D.A.V.M.S.)	
"	25.11.18.		Infantry A, B, C, & D. Cos. 35th M.T. Coys. exhibits possibly known. Few casualties; however shortage of own horses.	

WAR DIARY
INTELLIGENCE SUMMARY.
(Erase heading not required.)

Army Form C. 2118.

Place	Date	Hour	Summary of Events and Information	Remarks and references to Appendices
HARLEBEKE	26/11/18		Inspected 104th Bde, Bde. 104, 105, candidates passed. 19th, 19th; H. to B. commands on first examination, 1. to B. recommended for ability. Having not act to check & shortage of horses. 18th 7th & 19th D.L.I.; condition very good. 203rd P.L.R.E. condition poorly good. Remounts 2 Mules & 1 horse to M.V.T.	
"	27/11/18		Went information to V.G. & made enquiries to H.Q.'s M.V.T. re remount to MOULLE under orders to C.R.A. 35 Div. 106 Bde Group left for new area to-day.	
"	28/11/18		Moved with D.A.Q. to VOGELTE near POPERINGHE.	
"	29/11/18		35 Div. proceeding to ST OMER area by route march.	
"	30/11/18		Proceeded to EPERLEGQUES. with D.A.Q.	

1/12/18.

W.H. Taylor, Major A.V.C.
D.D.V.O. — 35 Div.

9

H.Q., 35TH DIVISION (GENERAL STAFF).	D.A.D.V.S. 35TH DIVISION.
No. G.227/3	No. 1
Date 1/1/19	Date 1-1-19

Ad. 2 to
35 Div.

Herewith "Diary" for Dec. 1918.

O.A.Q.
1.1.19

W. P. Taylor Major R.A.V.C.
D.A.D.V.S. 35 Div.

Army Form C. 2118.

WAR DIARY of D.A.D.V.S. 35° Div.

INTELLIGENCE SUMMARY. Vol. XII.
1.12.18 to 31.12.18.

(Erase heading not required.)

Summary of Events and Information

Place	Date	Hour	Summary of Events and Information	Remarks and references to Appendices
EPERLECQUES	1.12.18		Arrangements with Area Commandants at MOYELLE for billets for H.S. MN.T.	
"	2.12.18		Reports with begin & majority of animals with following units :— 17° Royal Scots; inoculated 1. R. with mange. 1.R.E. teams & 1. M.D. for mange the necessary contraction for disinfection to take place in — 12. N.G.T.; inoculated 1. L.D. Mule for tumour to shoulder. 106. L. C. A.S.C.; inoculated 1. N.9 for officers & 1.N.9 for theopied animal. 107. J. Ambulance; inoculated 1.N.9 for Strictly & Mounts watering. 205 J.C. R.E. Two mules & mare inoculated.	
"	3.12.18		Found two fields for Remounts to move to Division to selection by Board summer committee on 6° & 7° December.	
"	4.12.18		Reports 20 H. V.C.R.E. Mules punk form: 1. Rider found with Mange & evacuated to M.V.1. All precautionary measures taken to prevent spread the same, these inoculated. Plants in isolation for observation 35 Remount C. mules punk form.	

Army Form C. 2118.

WAR DIARY
or
INTELLIGENCE SUMMARY.
(Erase heading not required.)

Instructions regarding War Diaries and Intelligence
Summaries are contained in F. S. Regs., Part II.
and the Staff Manual respectively. Title pages
will be prepared in manuscript.

Place	Date	Hour	Summary of Events and Information	Remarks and references to Appendices
EPERLECQUES	4.12.18		45' M.T.J. arrived into their new area at MOULLE. Infantry into their billets.	
"	5.12.18		Capt. C.P. Thompson reported sick & confined to his billet. Weekly conference of V.Os.	
"	6.12.18		Presiding weapon committee completed all moves of Div. Res Artillery. Metcalfe presides.	
"	7.12.18		Attended parade to Presiding Manor from Artillery Units & 15 Division. Inspected with remarks to 45' M.V.S. for examination.	
"	8.12.18		Checked transport documents to OC 45' M.T.J. to state & found its urgent transport down river came at 204 R.E. & immediate return to M.T.T. for transport.	
"	9.12.18		Inspected 157 Bde R.F.A. Command under rotation with remounts Horn. Examined about 39 animals for debility & blindness, emphysema farriery, feed.	

Army Form C. 2118.

WAR DIARY
or
INTELLIGENCE SUMMARY.

(Erase heading not required.)

Instructions regarding War Diaries and Intelligence Summaries are contained in F. S. Regs., Part II. and the Staff Manual respectively. Title pages will be prepared in manuscript.

Place	Date	Hour	Summary of Events and Information	Remarks and references to Appendices
EPERLECQUES	10.12.18		Inspected 159 Fd. R.F.A. Ammunition. Ammunition presently good. Ready for Demobility & others for Blighters.	
"	11.12.18		Inspected with 2nd A.S.M.V.T. 1 Pecher belonging to 107 F Amb. reported with rear spring. Arranged new one then sent officer to see mode of arrange. Arranged instructed. Inspected No 1 C.A.S.C. Ammunition presently good. Truck floor to shelters requires attention. " 167 & 210 M.O.W. Co. Ammunition 1.29 from 167 & for Demobility	
"	12.12.18		Inspected 105 Fd. Ambulance. Ammunition presently good. Went of inspection of V.Co.	
"	13.12.18		Inspected with command at A.S.M.V.T. 55" Signal Co. Ammunition presently good.	
"	14.12.18		Inspected 19 M.E. Ammunition presently good.	

Army Form C. 2118.

WAR DIARY
or
INTELLIGENCE SUMMARY.
(Erase heading not required.)

Instructions regarding War Diaries and Intelligence Summaries are contained in F. S. Regs., Part II. and the Staff Manual respectively. Title pages will be prepared in manuscript.

Place	Date	Hour	Summary of Events and Information	Remarks and references to Appendices
EPERLECQUES	15.12.18		Inspected 20 H. F. C. R.E. two cases of amputates away amputated. Cases do not appear to be serious. Animals inspected for further examination.	
"	16.12.18		Inspected 105 Bty., R.A. Condition very good. All animals under cover.	
"	17.12.18		Inspected sick animals at 45 M.V.T. for examination to hospital.	
"	18.12.18		Arrived in Zeijeyem to Div. Train lines. At transport inspection. General statements & condition of animals very good.	
"	19.12.18		Arrived in Zeijeyem to Field Ambulance at transport inspection. General statements & condition of animals very good. Weekly conference at V.G.	
"	20.12.18		Inspected sick at 45 M.V.T. for examination. Witness transport Court Petzion.	

Army Form C. 2118.

WAR DIARY
or
INTELLIGENCE SUMMARY.
(Erase heading not required.)

Instructions regarding War Diaries and Intelligence Summaries are contained in F. S. Regs., Part II. and the Staff Manual respectively. Title pages will be prepared in manuscript.

Place	Date	Hour	Summary of Events and Information	Remarks and references to Appendices
EPERLECQ	21.12.18		Received O.O.N°1 I Army Warie N.D. V/1.21 dated 20.12.18. D for Capt. R.J. Stether R.A.V.C. to proceed to 17th Cdy for duty. Capt. J.B. Rennoldr R.A.V.C. to take over command of 45th M.V.S. Formal instructions accordingly.	
"	22.12.18		Major Capt. J.B. Rennoldr a/c M.V.S. & arranges for hour to take over command to the Stather relves. Capt. R.J. Stether render orders to proceed to 11th Cdy.	
"	23.12.18		Inspected A. Battery 157 Bde R.F.A. Condition generally good. is unit evacuates for hours condition. Capt. R.N. Stather R.A.V.C. proceeds to 11th Cdy for duty.	
"	24.12.18		Inspected 35th D.A.C. N°1 & 2 Sections under cover. 75% of N°.3. Section in the open. Condition to animals generally good.	
"	25.12.18		Visited 45th M.V.S. & inspected Mann demain in.	

Army Form C. 2118.

WAR DIARY
or
INTELLIGENCE SUMMARY.
(Erase heading not required.)

Instructions regarding War Diaries and Intelligence Summaries are contained in F.S. Regs., Part II. and the Staff Manual respectively. Title pages will be prepared in manuscript.

Place	Date	Hour	Summary of Events and Information	Remarks and references to Appendices
EPERLECQUES				
			Weekly conference of V.C., Inspector 20th & 4th W, R.E. & committee 2 R. & 1 & 8 horses on leave with prisoner unit of transport. Three animals had slaughter wounds.	
"	27.12.16		Inspected B, C, & D Batteries 157 Bde R.F.A. & C.C. Bde. Condition: young ponies. Turns arrival of B & D Batteries in the open. Few casualties & very little sickness among the animals.	
"	28.12.16		Inspected 159 Bde R.F.A. Condition: good cond. C. Bty standing very bad, condition inferior. Took M.M. transport inspector for duty & in attendance to 159 Bde R.F.A.	
"	29.12.16		Arranged to programme for inspection & Veterinary disinfection of all animals in the Division, to commence on 30th inst.	
"	30.12.16		Classified all animals belonging to H.Q. 159 Bde R.F.A., & A, & C Batteries.	
"	31.12.16		Classified all animals belonging to B & D Batteries 159 Bde R.F.A.	

WAR DIARY of D.A.D.Vet. 35th Div.
INTELLIGENCE SUMMARY

Army Form C. 2118.

Vol. 1. from 1-1-19 to 31-1-19

Place	Date	Hour	Summary of Events and Information	Remarks and references to Appendices
EPERLECQUES	1.1.19		Examined & classified all animals in Adv. 2t. D.A.C., No. 2 & 3 Sections.	
"	2.1.19		Examined & classified animals in charge of No. 1. Section D.A.C. & No. 1. Co. A.T.C.	
"	3.1.19		Veterinary Board examined & classified animals in charge of 35 Div. A.H.Q. & A. & B. Batteries 159 Bde. R.F.A.	
"	4.1.19		Veterinary Board examined & classified animals in charge of No. 2 Co. 159 Bde. R.F.A., C. & D. Batteries 159 Bde.	
"	5.1.19		Veterinary Board examined & classified animals in charge of 104 Rfg. Bde.; 203 ½ C.R.E. & No. 4. Co. Div. Train.	
"	6.1.19		Veterinary Board examined & classified animals of 106 Bfg. Bde.; 205 ½ C.R.E. & No. 4. Co. A.T.C.	
"	7.1.19		Veterinary Board examined & classified animals of 105 F. Ambc.; 35 Bn. M.G. Corps. No. 3. Co. Div. Train.	

Army Form C. 2118.

WAR DIARY
or
INTELLIGENCE SUMMARY.
(Erase heading not required.)

Instructions regarding War Diaries and Intelligence Summaries are contained in F. S. Regs., Part II. and the Staff Manual respectively. Title pages will be prepared in manuscript.

Place	Date	Hour	Summary of Events and Information	Remarks and references to Appendices
EPERLECQUES.	8.1.19		Veterinary Board examined & classified animals belonging to 105' Fld. Coy. R.E., 107' Fd. Amb., 19' Corps School.	
"	9.1.19		Veterinary Board examined & classified animals belonging to 35' D.A.C., C.R.E., M.M.P., 204 F.C.R.E. & 35' Depend'd Bn; 19' Withdrawal Provision. This completes the classification for 35' Divn.	
"	10.1.19		Reported mules at 45' M.V.T. who were branded knock-kneed from repatriation to England.	
"	11.1.19		15. Mules for repatriation sent to 45' M.V.T. from 101 M.T. Coy.	
"	12.1.19		Routine.	
"	13.1.19		Repatriation mules examined at 45' M.V.T. for evacuation to Britain.	
"	14.1.19		Attended a conference of D.D.V.S. at Corps H.Q. Capt. F.B. Pennett to do duty during absence on leave from 15 to 29 January (L.I.)	

(2)

Army Form C. 2118.

WAR DIARY
or
INTELLIGENCE SUMMARY.
(Erase heading not required.)

Instructions regarding War Diaries and Intelligence Summaries are contained in F.S. Regs., Part II. and the Staff Manual respectively. Title pages will be prepared in manuscript.

Place	Date	Hour	Summary of Events and Information	Remarks and references to Appendices
EPERLECQUES	15.1.19		Proceeded on 14 days leave to U.K.	
"	16.1.19		Attended Remount Parade for disinfection of 45" M.V.S. Horses.	
"	17.1.19		Arranged for collection and disposal of D. animals in Division in both troops attached.	
"	18.1.19		Mallenia Z animals in 107 F. Ambulance & 45" M.V.S.	
			Visited 221 P.O.W.C. Inspected 104 F. Amb.	
"	19.1.19		Inspected Mallenia animals in 107 F.Amb. & 45" M.V.S. 16 mentioned	
			Mallenia & 7 animals at 19 N. Gordon.	
			Classified 6 horses to C.D.A. H.T. Co. att. Entire Purchase Board & animals at B. Army Farm.	
"	20.1.19		Inspected 19 N.F. animal.	
			Mallenia M.M.P. 35 Div. H.Q. & 35" Regpd Co. Z animals.	
"	21.1.19		Collected, branded & malleined "D" animals at 45" M.V.S.	

Army Form C. 2118.

WAR DIARY
or
INTELLIGENCE SUMMARY.

(Erase heading not required.)

Instructions regarding War Diaries and Intelligence Summaries are contained in F. S. Regs. Part II. and the Staff Manual respectively. Title pages will be prepared in manuscript.

Place	Date	Hour	Summary of Events and Information	Remarks and references to Appendices
EPERLECQUE	22/1/19		Reports & despatches "B" arrived at H.5" M.V.T. Visited No. 1. G. Prison & 210. P.O.W. C.	
"	23.1.19.		Multiplied No. 1 G. Prison. Z. arrived Cathammarfin & A.H.D. C.A.A.H. by ctc. Town Mayor Wattin.	
"	24.1.19		Inspected No. 1. G. Prison Z. Prison. No reactions.	
"	25.1.19.		Inspected 7 arrivals at 19. N. Fr.	
"	26.1.19.		Inspection arrivals at D.N.O.9 & 35" Imperial G.	
"	27.1.19		Withdrawal 210. P.O.W. G. arrivals. Visited 107. Y. Ambl. & No. 1. G. Prison.	
"	28.1.19		Inspected 210 P.O.W. arrivals under Mullin Pert.	
"	29.1.19		Returns from Prison to O.K.	
"	30.1.19.		Reports arrivals from Prison to H.O.V.T. & took over duties from Capt. J.B. Pennath. I.R. Inspected 35" Imperial G.	
"	31.1.19.		Inspected 204 F.G. R.I.B. & 35" Imperial G. I.R. Inspected to carry on Z.O.H. G.	

W.M. Taylor. Major R.A.V.C.
Dated 31/1/19. "B" Dir.

Army Form C. 2118.

WAR DIARY of D.D.V.S. 35th Div.
or
INTELLIGENCE SUMMARY
Vol. II. 1.2.19 to 28.2.19.

(Erase heading not required.)

Instructions regarding War Diaries and Intelligence Summaries are contained in F. S. Regs., Part II. and the Staff Manual respectively. Title pages will be prepared in manuscript.

H.Q. 35TH DIVISION (GENERAL STAFF). No. G.122/5 Date 1/3/19

Place	Date	Hour	Summary of Events and Information	Remarks and references to Appendices
IEPERLEEQUE	1.2.19		Routine.	
"	2.2.19		Inspected 45th M.V.S. along with A.D.V.S. XIX Corps.	
"	3.2.19		Inspected 3rd Div. M.O animals	
"	4.2.19		Confined to Room	
"	5.2.19		to Evacuated to hospital	
"	6.2.19		Duties taken over by O.I.C. H.Q. M.V.S.	
"	7.2.19		Visit Staging Camp NORDAUSQUES	
"	8.2.19		Visit H.Q. M.V.S.	
"	9.2.19		" Routine	
"	10.2.19		"	
"	11.2.19		Visit Rly Horse Games 19.N.7.10 Jet Artemeren & 45th M.V.S. Seeing D.A.D.V.S. referent	
"	12.2.19		45th M.V.T inspected by D.D.V.S. and A.D.V.S.	
"	13.2.19		Visited 45th M.V.S. attended funeral of Col. D.A.D.V.S.	
"	14.2.19		Visited and inspected 10th Huf Belle on BEAUMARAIS.	
"	15.2.19		Visited 45th M.V.S. and 35 Divn Train.	
"	16.2.19		" " Staging Camp NORDAUSQUES	
"	17.2.19		Visited Section inspected 5th Armoury 35 Divn Train and 210 P.O.W.	
"	18.2.19		" " Inspected 204 fee Cay R.I. and 10 Corps Selective Animals	
"	19.2.19		Inspected 35 Divn Sign al Cy.	
"	20.2.19		Visited Section and 107 Jet Ammunen	
"	21.2.19		Visited Armoury of 35 Am. H.Q. & JAMSPETTE and 45 M.V.S	
"	22.2.19		duties of D.D.V.S. 35 Div Majr J.D. Richardson M.C. R.A.V.C. Assumed & tock on duties of F.B. Amorall Cerep In Sharp

WAR DIARY of D.A.D.V.S. 35 D.V.N.

INTELLIGENCE SUMMARY.

(Erase heading not required.)

Army Form C. 2118.

Instructions regarding War Diaries and Intelligence Summaries are contained in F. S. Regs., Part II. and the Staff Manual respectively. Title pages will be prepared in manuscript.

Place	Date	Hour	Summary of Events and Information	Remarks and references to Appendices
EPERLECQUES.	23-2-19		Took over duties of D.A.D.V.S	
	24-2-19		Inspected 35 Dn Stff Animals	
	25-2-19		Inspected Animals of No 1 Coy Div Train & 204 Fd Co R.E.	
	26-2-19		Inspected animals of 109 Fd Amb & 19 N.F. A.D.V.S visited office	
	27-2-19		Review. Evacuated to 40th Hospital. Handed over duties to O.C. 45th M.V.S.	
	28-2-19		Inspected Animals of 105 Infantry Bde	

Rumbure
N B Caystaury
(34)

D.A.D.V.S.
35TH DIVISION.

Army Form C. 2118.

D.A.D.V.S.
35TH DIVISION
No. S.57.
Date 1-4-19

Vol 34

WAR DIARY
or
INTELLIGENCE SUMMARY.
(Erase heading not required.)

Instructions regarding War Diaries and Intelligence Summaries are contained in F. S. Regs., Part II. and the Staff Manual respectively. Title pages will be prepared in manuscript.

Place	Date	Hour	Summary of Events and Information	Remarks and references to Appendices
EPERLECQUES	1-3-19		Visit Turn at ST OMER	
	2-3-19		Aumrau Parade of Divisional Train	
	3-3-19		Visit 1/35 Divn Train. Attended conference at D.H.Q. re distribution of Canteen Funds	
	4-3-19		Visit Horses	
	5-3-19		Visit 35th Signal Coy. XIX Corps School. 204 P.B. 19th INF and 210 P.O.W.	
	6-3-19		Visit M.V.S.	
	7-3-19		Visit 107 Field Ambulance	
	8-3-19		Visit charity avenue 221 P.O.W.	
	9-3-19		Visit M.V.S.	
	10-3-19		Visit 204 Fd Coy R.E. 105 Inf Bde and NORDAUSQUES Staging Camp	
	11-3-19		Visit M.V.S.	
	12-3-19		Visit D.A.E. and 210 P.W.	
	13-3-19		Visit 105 Inf Bde and NORDAUSQUES Staging Camp	
	14-3-19		Visit M.V.S.	
	15-3-19		Reading	

Army Form C. 2118.

D.A.D.V.S.
35TH DIVISION.
No ....
Date ....

WAR DIARY
or
INTELLIGENCE SUMMARY.
(Erase heading not required.)

Instructions regarding War Diaries and Intelligence Summaries are contained in F. S. Regs., Part II. and the Staff Manual respectively. Title pages will be prepared in manuscript.

Place	Date	Hour	Summary of Events and Information	Remarks and references to Appendices
EPERLECQUES	16.3.19		Visit 107 Fd Ambulance.	
	17.3.19		Visit XV Corps Vety. and 105th Fd Bty H.Q.	
	18.3.19		Visit (Section) Mobile Vety at ST OMER.	
	19.3.19		Visit E. EPERLECQUES CHATEAU.	
	20.3.19		Visit to 157 Bde. R.F.A.	
	21.3.19		Routine inspection work	
	22.3.19		Visit Mob. Vet. Section at ST OMER	
	23.3.19		Visit 2nd P.O.W. Camp 15th M.F.	
	24.3.19		Visit 106 Inf. Bde. at Tincques	
	25.3.19		Visit Mob. Vety. Section at ST OMER.	
	26.3.19		Visit 107 Fd. Ambulance and 135 Divn. Train	
	27.3.19		Recon. orders to attack 45th Inf Corps & No. Coy Div Train Ammunition Motors. Reconnaissance.	
	28.3.19		Despatches Lieut Crawford V.O.1k. 105 Bde R.F.A. & 62nd Divn in Capt. Thompson arrived at OTSD & tells me duties of D.A.D.V.S. D.A.D.V.S. Other works to Toll Dues. Hand over to Capt F.J. Thompson.	

WAR DIARY
or
INTELLIGENCE SUMMARY.
(Erase heading not required.)

Army Form C. 2118.

Place	Date	Hour	Summary of Events and Information	Remarks and references to Appendices
Tilleques.	30.3.19		completion of taking over duties of D.A.D.V.S. 84 & 5th M.V.S. and 45th M.V.S. were attached to Div. 1. Day 35th Reid. Train W.g.'s at 35th Reid. Train W.g.'s at Til 2 8 W.S. officers at B.12. Billets.	
"	31.3.19.		Capt. P.B. Russell 35th Div. sent on leave & relieved was despatched to 34th Div. sent and arrived at returning into D.A.D.V.S, 35th Div.	

D.A.D.V.S.
35TH DIVISION.
No. 224
Date 31.1.19

P.B.Russell
Capt. R.A.V.C.
for D.A.D.V.S.
35th Div.

Army Form C. 2118.

WAR DIARY

D.A.D.V.S. 35 DIVN

INTELLIGENCE SUMMARY.

(Erase heading not required.)

Place	Date	Hour	Summary of Events and Information	Remarks and references to Appendices
Tilques	1/4/19		Capt. Rennell, R.A.V.C. left to join 34 Div. Army of Occupation. Units visited 105 Field Ambulance Wattern, No 2 vy Cavy 35th Divn Train loaded Steele. 2" of snow in morning.	
do.	2/4/19		The first Unit of the Divn. to leave in cadre to Eng. 3 Batty 159 Bde R.F.A. entrained at Wattern.	
do.	3/4/19		Units visited 35th Revl Train. Reserve (Aug.) 1 35th Divn Train.	
do.	4/4/19		Capt. Taylor R.A.V.C. to 4 Animal Staying Camp(35th Div) proceeded to take over duties as D.A.D.V.S. to 31st Div. Major Matthews went to Ma.V.C. to command No 2. Vety Hosptl. 15-9. Bdr entrained at Wattern. No (Cadre Emptymnt)	
do.	5/4/19		Units visited 104 Bde Area Comm. (Budel & Steele) 105 Field Amb- Wattern, 2 & J. Cavy 35th Divl Train (Loaded on Steele)	
do.	6/4/19		Called to see horse at Army Artillery School Tilgues, colic. Another Convis this att. 19 Army Aux. Horse Coy. Tilg.ues, at arrival.	
do.	7/4/19		I gave orders to French Gdr. for animal att. to 35th Div. Col. Johnson D.C. Durin. reptd. to take up duties as A.D.V.S. Yorks.	
do.	8/4/19		Visited D.H.Q. 12 M.	
do.	9/4/19		Visited 19 Army Aux Horse Coy. 1 case H.D. fracture Tibia Destroy. Rain	
do.	10/4/19		Visited 2 Horse Hospd. 35th D.R.E. & 19 Army Aux. H. Coy. 1 H.D. Khird Conjunt. Temp 10	
do.	11/4/19		Went to St Omer, Could Aquired Ac. §45 M.V.S. visited 210 P.O.W. Coy. (2 by Cavy Divin. at Lederer 33 x L2. (Watt.W)	
do.	12/4/19		Went to football match 106 & 105 Inf. Bde. 106 won 2-1.	
do.	13/4/19		Cold evening visited 106 Inspect. (9 horses at 92 of ws) and 35 Battn M.G. Corps.	

Army Form C. 2118.

WAR DIARY
or
INTELLIGENCE SUMMARY.
(Erase heading not required.)

Instructions regarding War Diaries and Intelligence Summaries are contained in F.S. Regs., Part II. and the Staff Manual respectively. Title pages will be prepared in manuscript.

Place	Date	Hour	Summary of Events and Information	Remarks and references to Appendices
Tilques	14/4/19.		Visited by A/DADVS. 31st Div. Cav. Taylor, visited 104 Inf Bde. 106 Inf Bde. The latter sent 12 Annex's & Aygres	
do.	15/4/19.		visited 35th Field Amm & 106 Bde & 203 & 205 Coys R.E.	
do.	16/4/19.		visited by A.D.V.S. Corps, rec. orders to close officer	
do.	17/4/19.		B DADVS 3 & 5 Div rec. movement orders & proceed to U.K. to W.O.	

D.A.D.V.S.
35TH DIVISION.
No. 874.
Date 20.4.19

R.P. Humphreys
Capt. R.A.V.C.
D.A.D.V.S.
35th Divis

www.ingramcontent.com/pod-product-compliance
Lightning Source LLC
Chambersburg PA
CBHW080913230426
43667CB00015B/2666